ORGANIZED RELIGION AND SENIORS' MENTAL HEALTH

Anthony J. Blasi

University Press of America,® Inc.
Lanham • New York • Oxford

Copyright © 1999 by
University Press of America,® Inc.
4720 Boston Way
Lanham, Maryland 20706

12 Hid's Copse Rd.
Cumnor Hill, Oxford OX2 9JJ

Library of Congress Cataloging-in-Publication Data

Blasi, Anthony J.
Organized religion and seniors' mental health / Anthony J. Blasi.
p.   cm.
Includes bibliographical references and index.
1. Aged—Mental health—Religious aspects. 2. Psychology and
religion. 3. Mental health—religious aspects. 4. Experience
(Religion)—Psychological aspects. I. Title.
RC455.4.R4B55 1999 618.97'689—dc21   99—11322 CIP

ISBN 0-7618-1347-0 (cloth: alk. ppr.)
ISBN 0-7618-1348-9 (pbk: alk. ppr.)

♾™ The paper used in this publication meets the minimum
requirements of American National Standard for Information
Sciences—Permanence of Paper for Printed Library Materials,
ANSI Z39.48—1984

Table of Contents

Page

List of Tables

Preface

Ch. 1 Elders' Well-Being   1

Ch. 2 Making and Unmaking Personhood   23

Ch. 3 Problems in Later Years   31

Ch. 4 Religion as a Resource   43

Ch. 5 Ambivalence Over Religion   57

Ch. 6 What Churches Do   67

Ch. 7 Overview   95

Appendix One: Religion Moderating Depression   103

Appendix Two: Sample and Method in the Study of   107
      Ministers to Older Persons

Index of Names and Sources   115

Index of Topics   116

List of Tables

Page

1.1: Median Incomes of Householders, by Age   6

1.2: Percentage Below Poverty Level (1989 Income)   6

1.3: Household Income and Household Composition (1990)   7

1.4: Percentages Having Selected Ranges of Income, 1990   8

1.5: People per 1,000 Needing Help in Home Management Activities   12

1.6: Most Frequent Chronic Medical Conditions among Older People   13

3.1: Depression Symptom Scale Means By Medical Problems   36

3.2: Depression Symptom Scale Means By Financial Stress   37

3.3: Depression Symptom Scale Means By Stressful Life Events   38

3.4: Depression Symptom Scale Means By Perceived Social Support Scores   39

3.5: Perceived Social Support Scale Means By Problems   40

4.1: Public Religion By Perceived Social Support and Depression Symptoms   50

4.2: Perceived Social Support and Private Religiosity   52

4.3: Depression Symptoms and Private Religiosity   52

6.1: Per Cent of Total Adherents   69

6.2: Census Tract Income Per Capita Means   71

6.3: Denominational Breakdowns - Population and Samples   72

6.4: Distribution of Congregations among Tradition Types   76
       in the Nashville Sample

6.5: Distribution of Congregations among Types of   77
       Denominational Polity, By Tradition Types

6.6: Older Persons in Sampled Nashville Congregations   79

6.7: Census Tract Income Per Capita Means By Kinds of   81
       Older Persons' Problem Brought to Ministers

6.8: Full- and Part-Time Ministers to Older Persons   85

6.9: Seek Rate By How Often Older Persons Bring   86
       Problems

6.10: Seek Rate By Population Context and Tradition Type   87

6.11: Educational Attainment and Percentage in Senior   88
       Pastors' Residential Census Tract with 16+ Years
       Education, By Advisor of Minister to Older Persons

6.12: Congregations' Class Indicators By What Ministers to   89
       Older Persons Did When Problems Were Brought

to Them

A-1: Mean Scores of Principal and Demographic Variables   105
       By Race

A-2: Standardized Regression Coefficients (Dependent   106
       Variable = Perceived Social Support)

A-3: Standardized Regression Coefficients (Dependent   106
       Variable = Depression Symptoms)

A-4: 1990 Per Capita Income of Church Census Tracts.   110
       Predominantly Majority Congregations

A-5: 1990 Per Capita Income of Church Census Tracts.   111
       Predominantly African American Congregations

A-6: Mean Per Capita Income of Census Tracts of Pastors'   112
       Residences (Predominantly White Congregations -
       Total Known Population)

A-7: Mean Per Capital Income of Census Tracts of Pastors'   113
       Residences (Predominantly African American
       Congregations - Total Known Population)

Preface

The origin of this little book is quite simple. Professor Baqar A. Husaini of the Tennessee State University Center for Health Research asked me to collaborate with him on a study of mental health service utilization by older people in Tennessee. My part of the work was conducting an interview survey of individuals who undertook ministries to older people in the Nashville churches. After the interviews were completed and the information analyzed, I was to draft a report on the findings that would be distributed to the people who were interviewed. The general intention, under the guidelines of the federal Health Care Finance Administration, was to communicate what was learned back to the local community. The actual interviews took place during 1997; the information that was gathered seemed significant enough to be communicated beyond the few hundred people interviewed and beyond Nashville. I thought it useful to add further information for context - from the 1990 United States Census, the National Center for Health Statistics, and an earlier 1990 Nashville study of older people conducted by Professor Husaini.

The resultant report that this volume embodies accounts for limited aspects of the lives of older people in Nashville; it probably reflects on the life situations of similar people elsewhere in the United States. It describes in non-technical language the roles that churches play in older people's lives. While I have the general reader in mind, I try to avoid "talking down." I hope I have succeeded in striking the necessary balance between dwelling on issues of interest to specialists alone and simplification.

I am grateful to Baqar A. Husaini for the tables from his 1990 Nashville study, which he prepared at my request for use in this report. Any shortcomings in the use to which I put them, as well as the selection of the census and health information I use and the general discussion and conceptual formulations, are my responsibility. I am also grateful to Darrell A. Drumwright, Janice Emerson, and Joseph A.

Tam Lung for their assistance with the interviews in the 1997 study of Nashville ministers to older people. The project would not have gotten off the ground without the advice I received from Mary Strickland and Professor William Hardy, both of whom are very knowledgeable about the largely African American congregations in Nashville. I am especially indebted to the lay and clerical ministers themselves who serve the older people in Nashville's churches; they answered my questions patiently and candidly. Sharon Adkins was kind enough to read through the entire manuscript for me.

Finally, I wish to acknowledge the kind permission granted by the Glenmary Research Center, Nashville, Tennessee, for the use of some of their church membership data in Chapter 6.

Ch. 1 Elders' Well-Being

A reader who takes up a book like this one wants to know how good the typical experience of life is for older people, how that experience came to be as good or bad as it is, and what role church ministries may or actually do play in shaping such experiences of life. We do not want to confuse the account that follows by introducing our own ideas of how matters should be. What the role of religion in the subjective quality of life should be is an important matter, but it is simply not our present concern. We want to know how subjective well-being can be and is in fact enhanced for older people. We have no simple fixit program to sell; circumstances for individuals and for groups of people vary too much for a one-size remedy to fit all. In fact, if we succeed only in discovering and communicating how matters are and how they came to be that way, our success will not be a modest one. Life after sixty-five is an important concern today, and understanding what improves or detracts from it is correspondingly important. Consequently we will proceed carefully with what we have to say, abstaining from what people may be ready to hear us say simply because they hear many people say the same thing. We abstain from the verbal currency of pop-psychology - terms such as "self esteem" and "bonding."

We might all be tempted to buy into the eternal adolescence that is promoted by the advertising industry. There are lotions, creams, clothes, musics, exercise gadgets, and pills marketed on the premise that age is a condition to be delayed, wiped away, cured, or denied. The merchandisers need to make their livings, but we know better than to take their pitches at face value. Age brings problems with it, indeed; but it also brings opportunities. Age is not itself a problem to be denied, covered over, or cured, and the increasing presence of older adults in our world is not the real challenge either. It is the continued failure on our part as a society to include older adults within the pattern of life that is the real problem. At the very moment in history when older adults are increasingly present, trying to place them outside of everyday life represents a curious lapse of reasonability. It is this lapse that presents the real challenge, a lapse that would cede most of the everyday world to the pretense of omnipresent youth and would leave older adults at the margins of meaningful living.

In this book we describe the challenge presented by an unreasonable life pattern and the reasonable responses churches can provide in the face of that challenge. In many instances it is churches that prove to be the vital resource for help, albeit in ways that differ from denomination to denomination and congregation to congregation; they all differ significantly from community service agencies. Churches are not often accorded much attention; even many people who say they value religion as a personal interest think of churches as not being very important or as weak organizations that do not at all live up to the lofty ideals that they espouse. However, the role of churches in bringing balance and reason into people's daily lives can be significant. We will present findings from studies that were conducted in Nashville, Tennessee, a metropolitan area that is overwhelmingly Christian in its religious composition. We believe these studies will shed light on what churches and other religious organizations can do and actually do for the elderly, and with what effect. Before describing the problems that challenge older adults today, and before highlighting in later chapters the importance of churches in meeting these challenges, we need to consider the setting in which all this occurs.

Now More Than Ever

It is well known that greater numbers of people are living longer lives today than was the case in any previous era in history. This is especially true in advanced industrial societies such as the United States. It is this fact principally that makes it reasonable for us to reconsider our customarily inherited idea of the "life cycle" with its received wisdom that people "disengage" from society at some magical age and enter into a period of dependency. According to the United States Census reports[1] in 1970 almost one in ten Americans (9.9%) was aged sixty-five or over. By 1980 the ratio exceeded one in ten

(11.3%), and the population count published in the 1990 census reports an older population of 12.6% - all this before the "baby boom" generation has yet to reach the age of sixty. The quality of life of such a large and growing sector of the nation's population is obviously relevant to the quality of life of the whole society. The suggestion that such a large proportion of the population be disengaged seems on the face of it to be unreasonable.

A number of reasons can be found for the greater longevity of people living in technologically advanced societies at the present time. Among other factors, medical advances prevent early deaths from various sicknesses and conditions. Occupational safety measures also make a difference by preventing on-the-job deaths in the working population. Public health educational programs about the dangers from smoking tobacco and from excessive drinking, and about reasonable diets and regimens of exercise have enabled those people willing to heed the warnings to avoid early deaths. All of this adds up not only to living longer but doing so with some degree of health and vigor. The plain fact is that most people aged sixty-five and above are healthy enough not to live under care in nursing homes. Simple calculations from 1990 census information reveals that the vast majority of Americans aged 65-74 (98.2%) were living in households, not institutions; fully 89.2% of those aged 75 and above lived in households. Only some 1.8% and 10.8% of the two respective age groupings lived in some kind of group arrangement, including 1.4% and 10.1% respectively in nursing homes.[2]

It is interesting to look at such statistical information in a slightly different way. Out of the over eighteen million Americans aged 65-74 who comprise the 98.2% living in households, eleven and a half million (63.6% of the total population in the age bracket) are what the U.S. Census Bureau terms "householders" (owners of the home or person responsible for the rent). Similarly 67.5% of those aged 75-84 and 54.2% of those aged 85+ are householders. This suggests that the percentage living as the household head or, alternatively, living independently and alone *increases* in the seventies age grouping, probably because of the death of spouses, and then decreases toward 50% only in the eighties age grouping, probably because of changing the residence arrangements to live with other family members or in some group quarters. It is obviously necessary to think about the well-being of people in households, not exclusively about social services in medical settings, when considering the well-being of older persons in the United States and societies similar to it.

It becomes obvious upon examination of the facts that the needs of people, such as most of those in their sixties, who in many instances live as married couples, differ from those such as many of the septuagenarians, who often live alone. It is equally obvious that the needs of both of these differ from the needs of yet older individuals, who may need assistance in the day-to-day tasks of living. The challenges are various, not uniform, and the progression from one kind of challenge to another is neither inevitable nor likely to occur on a predictable schedule. Some couples live into their nineties. Because of medical problems some people need assistance in day-to-day living at a relatively early age. In addition, because widespread longevity is a relatively recent development, we have no received wisdom, no common knowledge for all to use. There is no traditional heritage that applies easily to a world like ours, in which life defies its traditional "cycle." Traditional wisdom does not deliver to us ready answers in this instance.

Personal Difficulties: Financial

Everyone knows that in contemporary industrialized societies money and property are significant factors in people's material well-being. The way of life of such societies requires a stream of income with which to purchase goods and rent or maintain residential quarters. For most people, the stream of income comes by way of earnings derived from gainful employment. Many people own or are paying off a mortgage on the property where they reside. Consequently the general pattern is for an income stream to cover all normal expenses when people rent their residential quarters, or for the income stream to cover all normal expenses except that proportion of the cost of housing which people may have paid off or may own outright as an asset. Medical expenses are covered largely under a "fringe benefit" insurance or health plan arrangement for some, or at a regularized group rate ("managed care") for others.[3] After age sixty-five and after the retirement from gainful employment that usually comes with that age, the income stream itself derives from a "fringe benefit" that had accumulated in previous years of work, any housing asset is likely to have been paid off, and medical expenses are covered in large part by the Medicare program.[4] The question arises, How good of an income stream does the variety of public and private pension schemes provide?

The most complete information about income in the United States comes from the decennial census, first set up for the purpose of allocating congressional districts among the states.   In order to appreciate the income information collected by the last census, it is necessary to think back to 1990, when it was taken, and recall how much someone had to earn to be satisfied as having a "good living" back then. What was good enough then would not be thought so today, even with inflation rates a good deal lower in the 1990s than they were before then. One way to interpret the 1990 Census information is to look at the income levels reported for the different age groupings. People in their teens and early twenties are paid poorly because they typically work at low-skill jobs or are taken on in "entry level" jobs in order to begin training in the skills needed in a line of work. People working in their late twenties and early thirties have not yet had time to "work their way up" into positions of greater responsibility and earning potential. How did the incomes of those sixty-five and older compare to the incomes of these and the other pre-sixty-five age brackets? The census data suggest that those sixty-five and above did not fare well (see Table 1.1).[5] Their median income was situated between that of the teenagers and people in their early twenties and that of those in their late twenties and early thirties. In terms of income, it was like beginning adulthood all over again.

While this income information is disconcerting, to say the least, it does not necessarily indicate a substandard quality of life. A householder aged sixty-five or above may have a working spouse whose earnings are added to the household income total. Alternatively, the individuals may be sharing their places of residence with their adult children or some other relatives. Such factors are taken into account when U.S. government data report percentages of "populations living below the poverty level" (see Table 1.2 for the 1990 data).[6] Social Security and other retirement benefits appear to have improved matters

Table 1.1: Median Incomes of Householders, by Age

Age of Householder	Median Income, 1990
15-24	$ 16,219
25-34	$ 31,497
35-44	$ 41,061
45-54	$ 47,165
55-64	$ 39,035
65+	$ 25,049

Table 1.2: Percentage Below Poverty Level (1989 Income)

Age	Married Couple Families	Living Alone
60-64	5.1%	24.6%
65-74	4.8%	22.6%
75+	7.7%	27.0%

Source: 1990 U.S. Census

slightly for people when they reached age sixty-five, insofar as the percentages below the poverty level went down from the 60-64 age bracket to the 65-74 one. However, the financial circumstances of the people who were living alone was much more often a problem than for the married couples; about a fourth of those living alone were living below the poverty line. The difference between the poverty rates of the older married couple households and those of older people living alone suggests that we really need to look closely at the compositions of households in general - not only whether older people live in them, but also whether all who live in them are older, how many live in the households, and what relationship the people are who live in them have to the older household members. One of the 1990 Census reports goes a long way toward doing this for us (see Table 1.3). The presence of a person aged sixty-five or above does not of itself seem to be related to a markedly lower income per person figure (right hand column in Table 1.3). However, except where an elder other than a spouse is

Table 1.3: Household Income and Household Composition (1990)

Composition	Median Income	Income Per Person
Without persons 65+	$33,774	$14,277
With persons 65+	$18,062	$13,814
All household members 65+	$14,143	$14,628
Householder or spouse 65+	$28,041	$13,272
Elder is a non-spouse relative	$43,304	$12,392
Elder is a non-relative	$34,667	$11,600

Source: U.S. Bureau of the Census, Money Income of Households, p.50.

living in a household, the sixty-five or above age category is related to lower median *household* incomes. This is to say that while the income streams of those sixty-five or older are lower they are usually divided among the expenses of a smaller number of persons. Income shortfalls are not characteristic in general of the entire older age group, but they are more common among older people who are living alone. As we saw above, their income streams more frequently leave them below the poverty level.

When considering median incomes, it is easy to lose sight of the fact that half of the population falls below the median figure.[7] Given the differences between the incomes of married couples and persons living alone and between those in the earlier older age brackets and those more advanced in years, the most accurate way to report the income situation is in a distribution table that gives separate figures for the "currently married" and those living alone and for the two age groupings (see Table 1.4). The largest percentage of married people aged 65-74 appear in the $15,000-24,999 income bracket, as did the largest percentage figure of married people aged 75 and above; the latter age grouping had higher percentages in the lower income brackets than did those aged 65-74. Among those living alone, the largest percentages had incomes in the $5,000-9,999 bracket, especially among those aged 75 and above.

When we turn to the sources of annual income for people aged sixty-five and older, we find that 92.1% of the almost thirty million

Table 1.4: Percentages Having Selected Ranges of Income, 1990

Income Range ($)	Married Couples		Living Alone	
	65-74	75+	65-74	75+
-4,999	1.7	2.7	15.9	18.9
5,000-9,999	6.2	11.3	31.9	39.4
10,000-14,999	11.2	17.8	18.5	16.0
15,000-24,999	25.6	27.4	18.7	13.8
25,000-34,999	19.1	15.5	7.4	5.4
35,000-49,999	16.5	11.8	[7.6]	[6.0]
50,000	+19.6	15.5	[merged with above]	

Calculated from U.S. Bureau of the Census, Social and Economic Characteristics, United States (Washington: U.S. Government Printing Office, 1993), p. 39.

older Americans in 1990 received some income from the Social Security retirement supplement program, but this source of income yielded a median income of only $6,163.[8] Social Security payments were an important part, but only a part, of older Americans' incomes. A large number, some 69.3%, had interest income as well, but this amounted only to a median annual yield of $3,805. Only 32.5% had pension income, yielding a median income contribution of $7,823. Small fractions of the older population had other kinds of income: 17.8% had dividend income (yielding a median contribution of $3,272); 16.5% had wages, salaries, and other earnings (median $14,146); 10% had rents, royalties, etc. (median $4,072); 6.8% had survivors' benefits (median $6,370); 5.3% were poor enough for SSI (median $2,199); 4% received veterans' benefits (median $3,361); and 1.0% received disability benefits ($8,329). As percentages of the population, those receiving other forms of income - unemployment compensation, workers' compensation, welfare for support of dependents, etc. - were negligible.

The small percentage (16.5) with earnings income can be deceiving because the base number includes many people in the higher age brackets. In fact, a much larger percentage continues in the labor force in the years immediately following their reaching the age of sixty five. There is no documentation of important but unpaid work done by people who are officially retired and not in the labor force. Some 27.9% of men aged 65-69 and 16.9% of women in the same age category were in the labor force in 1990. Only at age seventy and after do the percentages of people in the work force drop to 11.7 and 4.8 for men and women respectively.[9] It is simply not the case that nearly all people retire at age sixty-five.

While we can see the great diversity in financial circumstance that older Americans face, the relevant information is limited so far to dollars and cents figures. What do the individual people who live within these income levels think about them? How do they respond to them? Do they find their incomes sufficient? The U.S. Census does not collect that kind of information. However, in a study of older people in Nashville, Tennessee, undertaken at the Tennessee State University Center for Health Research, questions were asked about some of these matters.[10] The information was collected in 1990 in interviews with 969 people. Since one of the purposes of the original study was to make comparisons between African American and majority (or "white") older people, there were almost equal numbers of both racial groupings who were interviewed (498 whites and 497 African Americans). The interviews were following up earlier ones from two years before, with an original grouping of 1,200 randomly selected individuals.[11] Because the information collected in this study is so detailed, we will return to it in later chapters. Among other questions, the study participants were asked whether they were satisfied or dissatisfied with their family income. Sixty-six per cent of both men and women aged 65 to 69 were dissatisfied, as were 81.0% of men and women aged 70 or higher. Even more said they were highly dissatisfied with their standards of living - 88.7% of the men and 89.5% of the women under 70, 85.7% of the men and 93.1% of the women 70 or over. Just under 30% of the people interviewed in the Nashville study said they had actual money problems, and about 22% reported trouble paying bills. Just under 10% said they experienced stress related to financial problems. We get the general impression that many people were at the margin; they were getting by but would not have had the resources to handle a major expense.

Personal Difficulties: Medical

The most evident challenge to the older person is medical. Not all older persons are ill during most of their time after age sixty-five, but there are those who are, and most will experience illness at some time. Moreover, we would hardly be able to speak of satisfactory medical progress if people's life spans increased without their health being tolerable. Consequently we need to think in terms not only of life expectancy but also of health expectancy. At what age do people generally live free of permanent disability - i.e., free of limitations on their independently carrying out major day-to-day activities? Fortunately, this longevity of health has been increasing along with the life expectancy. While in 1964 men aged sixty-five could look forward to more than twelve more years of life, they could expect only about half of that many years of health in the sense of freedom from disability; women lived sixteen more years or so on the average, ten of those years free of disability. Two decades later in 1985 men aged sixty-five could expect to live between fourteen and fifteen more years on the average, over ten of those years free of disability; and women could expect to live eighteen to nineteen more years, over thirteen of them free of disability.[12] Current estimates say that men aged sixty-five in the year 2000 will live about sixteen more years on average, and women slightly over nineteen years.[13] A little calculation shows that in 1964 American men and women could anticipate on the average six years of disability before death but that by 1985 this was shortened to four or five years out of a life span that had increased about two additional years.

Not all disabilities limit people in the same way or to the same extent. In a ground breaking 1956 New York City study of 500 people sixty years of age and older, researchers asked those interviewed who had reported illnesses whether their illnesses limited them at all, kept them from work, kept them from doing things, kept them at home, and whether the illnesses kept them from seeing people. Only 14% of those with illnesses (8% of the total sample interviewed) said illnesses limited them in all the ways mentioned.[14] We would not expect the percentages reported in the 1956 survey to hold true today,[15] but the researchers' strategy of assessing medical conditions in terms of what illnesses may or may not prevent someone from doing was clearly to the point. At the end of the twentieth century, now that people enjoy not only longer life spans but also longer health spans, it is important to think in terms of what people over sixty-five can do for one another, how long on the average they can do it, and degrees to which different older people need what other senior citizens can do for them. Turning again to the 1990 U.S. Census and making simple calculations from its population characteristics reports, we find that only 8.3% of Americans aged 65 to 74 report self-care limitations, and only 15.3% of those aged 75and above report such limitations. It is evident that those able to help far out number those who need care, though because some kinds of care require the expertise of specialists not all those who are available can render every kind of care that may be needed.

We want to look more closely than the gross U.S. Census reports allow, at the kinds of limitation older people confront. Some very useful factual information appears in the 1984 National Health Interview Survey and published by the U.S. National Center for Health Staistics.   The interviewees, who did not include nursing home residents, were asked specific information about eleven areas of daily activity that different older people could or could not do for themselves without help from somebody (see Table 1.5). While a great majority appeared not to need any help in seven of the areas, a substantial minority needed assistance with four activities - light and especially heavy housework, shopping for personal items, and managing money, especially among women after age eighty-five. If we add up the persons per 1,000 needing help with the eleven activities in each age group and gender column, thus making a rough measure of how much people in each column need help in general, we can see that the figures really increase after age 85. How much people needed help did not seem to increase gradually with age but rather jumped at about that age.

One other important kind of general descriptive information that can be obtained is gathered by means of an extensive check-list of medical problems.   Simply asking about problems in general sometimes misses ones that are not on an interviewee's mind at the time of the interview, but by using a detailed listing of possible medical conditions it turns out that many people report three or more chronic medical conditions. In Table 1.6 the most frequent kinds of chronic medical conditions that older people report are listed, along with their incidence rate per thousand people. Obviously, people having such conditions are more likely to be the individuals who need assistance performinc some of the home maintenance activities. This should not

Table 1.5 People per 1,000 Needing Help in Home Management
Activities

Activity	Age 65-74		Age 75-84		Age 85 and Over	
	Men	Women	Men	Women	Men	Women
Heavy housework	72.0	131.8	113.2	235.1	249.6	462.7
Shopping	33.6	37.8	71.9	112.9	205.1	321.6
Bathing	33.4	36.7	68.1	88.8	194.9	227.9
Managing money	19.9	10.9	35.8	42.2	138.5	198.2
Light housework	22.5	23.7	49.9	60.1	121.4	191.3
Preparing meals	18.0	18.0	44.1	51.0	140.2	183.7
Dressing	32.5	26.8	56.6	47.3	126.5	135.7
Getting in/out bed/chair	17.4	17.9	28.8	41.8	------	99.1
Using telephone	10.6	6.9	28.5	19.9	94.0	98.3
Using toilet	13.6	11.4	22.7	33.4	------	95.3
Eating		8.5	4.7	17.6	13.9	-----
Column sums	282	327	537	746	1,270	2,014

Source: John Peter Fulton, et al., *Physical Functions of the Aged: United States, 1984. Vital and Health Statistics 10(7).* Washington: National Center for Health Statistics, 1989.

be seen as a general state of helplessness, however, since there are far more activities most can do without help than there are activities with which they need help. Judging from the U.S. Census information about self care cited above, what people typically need help with is not considered "self-care"; the latter would appear to fall within the category of what most older people can do for themselves.

Those older Americans who cannot provide for their own self-care often depend on nursing home services. When people need to change residential arrangements to nursing homes, they typically do so at age eighty for men and age eighty-three for women. What they most

Table 1.6 Most Frequent Chronic Medical Conditions among Older
People

Number of Chronic Conditions per 1,000 People

Condition	Age 65-74 Men	Women	Age 75 and above Men	Women
Arthritis	430.8	513.6	424.9	604.4
High blood pressure	307.7	395.8	339.2	417.5
Heart disease	319.3	299.4	429.9	361.4
Hearing impairment	298.8	238.0	447.1	307.8
Cataracts	79.0	192.4	214.7	259.2
Deformity/orthopedic	144.4	174.1	169.3	189.9
Chronic sinusitis	118.2	175.7	113.9	176.1
Visual impairment	78.4	75.5	79.0	110.7
Frequent constipation	13.8	71.5	60.2	102.2

Source: P.F. Adams and M.A. Marano, *Current Estimates from the National Health Interview Survey, 1994*. Washington: National Center for Health Statistics. *Vital and Health Statistics* 10(193), 1995, pp. 83-84.

frequently need help with in a nursing home that they cannot do for themselves is bathing or showering. The illness that is most frequently the primary reason for admission to nursing homes is disease of the circulatory system.[16] Simply because of the increasing life span, we would expect the percentage of all people over a fixed age such as sixty-five to have increased in recent decades. The same kind of reasoning would lead us to expect the proportion of the population at a higher yet age category to also go up; these are the people with self-care limitations. Thus as a matter of a simplistic kind of arithmetic, we would expect higher and higher proportions of all people aged above 65 to be nursing home residents. This is what the nursing home surveys generally showed from the 1970s to 1985. A 1973-74 survey found that 4.47% of Americans aged 65 and above lived in nursing homes; the figure increased to 4.71% by 1977 and leveled off to 4.62% in 1985. However, the figure was *down* to 4.13% in the 1995 survey. The reason for the recent decline is thought to be in part a healthier status of older people in general but also the availability of such alternatives to nursing homes as assisted living quarters and home health care services.

The 1990s especially have seen the growth of home health care services, which served 2.97% of the older Americans in 1992, 3.24% in 1993, and 4.16% (more than in nursing homes) in 1995. There are three obvious inferences to be drawn here: 1) There are increased numbers of older Americans having self-care limitations who need assistance; 2) The people needing assistance cannot be visited in groups in nursing homes but can only be visited in many cases in their non-group residences; and 3) There are increasing numbers of healthy older people who can visit and can help those who need assistance. The challenge is to mobilize those elderly who are healthy enough to provide this kind of service to the elderly who have chronic medical conditions, including depression.

Depression is a medical condition that often affects older people. We hear more about it now than in past years. Medical and mental health professionals have come to identify the condition more consistently in recent times, partly because of advances in their knowledge about it and partly because it is one of the illnesses that affect many people as they live longer than people generally did in the past. Depression is a combination of how someone feels, thinks, and acts; it is painful in its own way. It can begin with simple difficulties that cannot be controlled and worsen to the point of leading to confusion, uncooperativeness, and memory loss. Depression is not "senility." When the clinicians talk about depression, they have in mind a condition that can be treated. It may be present when certain symptoms are evident five or more days a week. These symptoms include the following:

1. Sadness, and looking sad; neglect of appearance; and
2. Four or more from this list:
   - Loss of appetite and weight, neglecting to prepare food or only eating one kind of food;
   - Difficulty in sleeping;
   - Physical agitation for a while, and then physical lifelessness;
   - Loss of pleasure or interest in activities, loss of sexual interest;
   - Fatigue, loss of energy;
   - Feeling worthless or guilty;

- Trouble concentrating, slowed thinking, indecisiveness;
- Thoughts of suicide; life does not seem worth living.

What is particularly interesting, and is something that we will explore in more detail in a later chapter, is that depression seems to be related to medical problems and financial worries and that in some cases it can be lessened in advance by some of the social support resources that the church congregations possess.

Other Life Stressors

A person's quality of life involves far more than physical and financial well-being. Any number of factors can occasion stress and worry. The individual may worry about the problems that other family members face. Rather than a source of support, in the worst of circumstances family members may be threatening and intimidating. Alternatively, the individual may simply be alone, with any family geographically distant or emotionally alienated. Sometimes, an individual's own line of conduct puts off family members and becomes increasingly problematic for them as the individual ages. We have no real social formula to tell us which problems faced by other family members should be of no concern to the older family member or how geographically close modern families should be. The resultant ambiguity leaves room for worry and stress and, sometimes, self-blame.

These "other" problems that originate in the relationships between the older person and others, especially between the individual and members of the family, frequently take the form of loneliness. Most frequently, however, the problem of loneliness comes not from such problematic behavior in the family but from the death of loved ones and friends. The feelings of loneliness become tied up in many instances with the resultant feelings of loss and grief. When a person's husband or wife is gone, there is little likelihood that other family members or friends can fit into the individual's life to the same degree or in the same way emotionally as did the deceased. Friends also begin to become incapacitated and die, and even one's children may do so as well. A lack of friends was cited as a problem by 30% of the men aged

65-69 in the Tennessee State University Nashville study, though only by approximately half that many (15.1%) by men aged seventy and over, and by only 17.1% of women aged 65-69 and 15.8% of women aged seventy and over. While men between sixty-five and seventy have the highest rate of citing a lack of friends as a problem, there seems to be a consistent 15% to 17% of men seventy and over and women of all the ages beyond sixty-four who need more friends. When phrased as a lack of a social life rather than a lack of friends, the percentages that emerge are a little less dramatic but point to the same reality; 22.5% of men under seventy, 10.6% of men seventy and over, 20.2% of women under seventy, and 14.7% of women seventy and over stated that a lack of a social life was a problem for them.

Resources to Cope with Life Stresses

It is interesting to compare the life situation of the young adult with that of the older person. The young adult may be just out of school and just out of home and not yet very wise about such matters as marriage, whom to consider as friends, and how to set up and maintain a household. Finances and medical insurance may be something of a mystery, with important decisions being delayed. Intellectually, the young adult may know that religion is supposed to be important, but so far it may seem useful only for very little children who need to be taught the basics of right and wrong. The older person similarly may be out of work and facing the prospect of the family experience changing greatly or disintegrating altogether toward the end of life. However, the older person is likely to be far wiser about marriage and friends and to know well how to set up a new household or maintain one. Only some, however, may be really astute about finances, since it may have been only one spouse who gained all the expertise related to taxes, investments, and real estate. The expertise people aged sixty-five and older develop in dealing with Medicare, medical insurance in general, and the medical establishment in general is often remarkable. Older persons are far more likely to know from experience the importance of religion in life; many may have resumed some involvement in church after a period of neglecting it and have experienced a difference between the feeling of something being missing and something being there that should be there. These differences between the young and the old are the practical side of what people have in mind when they speak of the "wisdom of age."

Not every older person will have the same reservoir of experience to draw on when needed. As already mentioned, not everyone develops expertise in financial matters. Moreover, it is not possible to produce companionship out of experience alone. How much a person is involved in an on-going social life, as opposed to being alone, varies. The social gerontologists have three separate ways of talking about this. Some speak of "social integration" and look at such facts as whether a person is currently married, whether the person is a member of a church, how available the person's family and friends may be, and whether the person participates in community organizations of one kind or another. Other gerontologists speak of "social networks" and look at who the people are who are present in one's network of associates, whether one's own relationships overlap with those of the other members of the network (e.g., have the same friends in common), and whether one associates with a particular other person for more than one kind of activity (e.g., not only church but entertainment as well). A third group of gerontologists speak of "social support" and look at whether there is emotional affect, admiration, respect, and affirmation in one's social environment, and whether there is instrumental help in the form of advice, information, and practical assistance at hand when the individual needs it.[17] All of these - social integration, social networks, and social support - vary. People enjoy more or less of each, and the form of what they enjoy varies as well.

Here we can only consider these matters in the most preliminary manner. We can begin with the fact that in 1990 some 49.6% of the 17,846,191 Americans aged sixty-five and above who lived in households (rather than in group quarters) lived as married couples. The balance (50.4%) lived without a spouse.[18] It would appear, then, that about half did not (and presumably about half still do not) enjoy one aspect of what the social gerontologists term "social integration." Apart from those living alone, there are those living with family other than a spouse, living with non-family in households, living in group arrangements, or living in nursing homes; these may enjoy social contacts that those living alone may not frequently have.

Church membership varies from having one's name in a register but rarely participating in the congregational life of the church, to being involved in a small church activity group several times a week. One may know and be known by the church officials well or hardly at all and similarly know and be known by other church members well or hardly at all. Even if one attends church worship services and participates in a church-centered social life, it remains an open question whether one had advanced in a spiritual life enough to have built up a repertory of interior skills or to have developed an adequate perspective in one's consciousness with which to face difficulties. Some "religious" people may have a child's kind of spirituality, still focusing on rather superficial notions of right and wrong and magically trying to make God do one thing or another. We will take up these issues in later chapters.

The Approach of the Book

The difficulties and resources we have been describing are not related in some mechanical way to older people's subjective well-being. They work through the individual's own life experiences. Faith and spirituality - or religion, in the favorable sense that many people use that term[19] - are significant factors in people's life experiences. The churches' ministries work with people, often aiming at people's self-empowerment and self-efficacy in the community. It is this dimension of older people's lives that we explore in the pages to follow. With respect to the particular subject of depression, we see it as oftentimes being a cluster of symptoms that may be organized into a condition. Medicines can control the physical causes and behavioral symptoms of depression, but where there are social causes as well, causes that allow health concerns and financial worries, for example, to dominate a person's life and consciousness, medication fails to address the whole problem.

Scientists have been gathering information in Nashville on many of these matters for years by interviewing older people. More recently we have been gaining insights from a different perspective by interviewing church people who engage in ministry to older persons. Some of the ministers to older persons are trained clergy, some are simply individuals who began to preach when they felt a call, some are non-clergy who found that they were good with older people, and some are older people themselves who worked regularly at their ministry as unpaid volunteers but who work with great energy and efficacy. One of the things all these people told us many times is that it is necessary to recognize and minister with (not necessarily "to") the whole person. We are taking our cue from the collective experience of these people.

In the next chapter we will describe the emergence of people's realization of themselves as whole persons, vulnerable to problems but also possessing the capacity to face problems. The capacity for religion will be shown to be an essential dimension of personhood. We will show how the sense of personhood can be threatened in people's later years. In Chapter 3 we will turn to the 1990 Nashville survey data to show what problems older people typically face and what consequences these problems have on their subjective well-being. Using the 1990 Nashville survey data again in Chapter 4, we show what role religion can play in mitigating the impact of difficulties among older people. Religious involvement can be made less effective, however, if people are ambivalent about religion. In Chapter 5 we explore how ambivalence over religion has come to be a normal experience in the contemporary world. In Chapter 6, on the basis of our 1997 interviews with ministers to older persons in Nashville, we draw a picture of church ministries for older persons and examine some of the specific actions that the ministers take when helping people confront difficulties in old age. Chapter 7 draws all these elements together into an overview.

Notes

1. Unless noted otherwise, census information is from Bureau of the Census, *1990 Census. Population Characteristics, United States* (Washington: U.S. Government Printing Office, 1991).

2. Grouping all nursing home residents together in a single category can be misleading. There are three major classes of nursing home care. In two classes, where the funding is more adequate, the care is paid for either by Medicare or, if long term, out of some long term care insurance or the patient's income and estate. If the patient begins with a large estate, it is possible to transfer it *in toto* to the institution and receive in exchange a comfortable level of care indefinitely; that is the first class. Alternatively in the second class, the long term patient pays from income, savings, and eventually the sale of property until impoverished. When all resources have been exhausted, the patient is transferred into the third class, which often involves a physical relocation; the funding is minimal, paid for by Medicaid. Most long term nursing home residents go through a career in which they begin under relatively comfortable conditions under Medicare or private funding and then,

when their assets have been "paid down," i.e., when they have been pauperized, they end up in the Medicaid coverage, where their Social Security checks go directly to the institution. The limited funding under Medicaid-funded nursing home care leaves patients to the mercy of moment-by-moment bureaucratic irrationalities and discomforts, despite the best efforts of harried and underpaid staff. For a sympathetic treatment, see Timothy Diamond, *Making Gray Gold. Narratives of Nursing Home Care* (Chicago: University of Chicago Press, 1992).

3. The connection between medical coverage and employment, especially employment with a large company, was a byproduct of governmental economic controls during World War II. The government imposed wage and price controls because of an anticipated wave of increases that would come about from the sudden war demand; unable to attract or hold onto workers with increased paychecks, companies resorted to including medical coverage in their compensation packages.

4. In 1995, the average total annual Medicare payments per beneficiary (i.e., per person who was hospitalized and was covered by the program) for hospitalization came to $6,364 while the average payment total by the beneficiaries was $551 - Health Care Financing Administration, *1997 Data Compendium* (Baltimore: U.S. Department of Health and Human Services, 1977), p. 73.

5. U.S. Bureau of the Census, *Money Incomes of Households, Families, and Persons in the United States: 1990* (Washington: U.S. Government Printing Office, 1991), p. 3. The median income figure used in Table 1.1 is the yearly income of the person at the middle, with half the population of householders earning more and half less than that person did.

6. In 1995, some 13.8% of the U.S. population lived below the poverty level (by one means of calculation) while the corresponding figure for the sixty-five and over population was 10.5% - Health Care Financing Administration, *1997 Data Compendium,* pp. 58 and 59.

7. The median is less deceptive than the "average" or mean, which can be made artificially high by the inclusion of a relatively small number of very rich individuals.

8. Data for this section are reported in or calculated from Bureau of the Census, *Money Income of Households*, p. 190. At the end of 1996, the average Social Security cash benefit came to $8,940 per year - calculated from Health Care Financing Administration, *1997 Data Compendium*, p. 57.

9. Percentages calculated from data reported in U.S. Bureau of the Census, *Census of Population. Social and Economic Characteristics, United States* (Washington: U.S. Government Printing Office, 1993), p. 33.

10. The Nashville data were gathered, beginning in 1988, under National Institutes of Health grants (RCMI) G12-RRO3033-01 and (MBRS) SO6-RRO8092-16, with support from the National Institute of Aging, to

Tennessee State University, Baqar A. Husaini, Principal Investigator. Most of the items of interest in the present context are from a 1990 wave of interviews. I wish to express my gratitude to Professor Husaini for making this information available.

11. In two years' time 231 of the original 1,200 respondents had either died, moved out of town, or had relocated without leaving a forwarding address.

12. J.M. Robine, C. Mathers, and N. Brouard, "Trends and Differentials in Disability-Free Life Expectancy: Concepts, Methods, and Findings," in G. Caselli and A.D. Lopez (eds.), *Health and Mortality Among Elderly Populations* (Oxford: Clarendon Press, 1996), pp. 182-201, at p. 194; Robine et al. based these conclusions from data reported by J.B. McKinlay, S.M. McKinlay, and R. Beaglehole, "A Review of the Evidence Concerning the Impact of Medical Measures on Recent Mortality and Morbidity in the United States," *International Journal of the Health Sciences* 19:2: 189-208. The life spans reported in these data are longer than the "average length of life" statistics authors usually write about because all those people who die before age 65, such as military personnel dying in combat, are not included in the averages.

13. Health Care Financing Administration, *1977 Data Compendium*, p. 55.

14. B. Kutner, D. Fanshel, A.M. Togo, and T.S. Langner, *Five Hundred Over Sixty. A Community Survey on Aging* (New York: Russell Sage Foundation, 1956), p. 125.

15. Twenty-three per cent of the ill (13% of the total number of respondents) were kept from work, 32% (18%) from doing things, 24% (13%) kept at home, 7% (4%) kept from seeing people.

16. These summary statistics are available on the internet at the National Center for Health Statistics web site. *Characteristics of Elderly Nursing Home Residents: Data From the 1995 National Nursing Home Survey. Advance Data 289.* National Center for Health Statistics, July 16, 1997.

17. P.A. Dykstra, *Next of (Non)Kin. The Importance of Primary Relationships for Older Adults' Well-Being* (Amsterdam: Swets & Zeitlinger, 1990), pp. 7-8.

18. Calculated from U.S. Bureau of the Census, *Social and Economic Characteristics*, p. 39.

19. Many theologically informed people take *religion* to be a negative term that refers to a wholly human creation rather than to faith. Others use the word interchangeably with *faith* and *spirituality*. This difference in usage was evident in our interviews in 1997 with ministers to older people in Nashville.

Ch. 2 Making and Unmaking Personhood

In the first chapter we collected some statistics that present the contexts in which older people in the United States typically live. That presentation only begins to tell the story since people's lives consist of more than their surroundings. In fact, by being attentive to what is around them, by seeing possibilities in what they find, and by constructing personal interpretations of the world around them, people fashion more or less individualized environments. These environments are as much subjective constructs as natural conditions, but that does not make them any less real in their consequences. They are comprised of what people take to be particularly relevant to their lives. Such environments are customized, so to speak, in that the importance of various environmental elements depends upon the way people pay attention to them and understand them.

We are all familiar with the business entrepreneur who sees opportunity where others do not, and we know that sculptors sometimes "see" a statue in a piece of rock that others take no interest in. On a more mundane level, there are people who collect and save scraps of metal and wood; their accumulations seem to serve no purpose until something needs to be repaired or reconstructed. The "junk" collector often has just the material needed, having seen possibilities for it all along. The environments that statistics reflect consist of similar possibilities; they depend upon the imaginations of the people who see or fail to see important possibilities in the conditions that the statistics reflect.

Our imaginations, which are responsible for the possibilities that our environments hold in store for us, are the mental mannerisms of our very personalities. We have become accustomed to seeing various ways of acting, and we have "internalized" them, i.e. imported them into the repertory of images available in our habitual thoughts. The impressions that have been with us since earliest childhood are still at work in our imaginations. The figures that we have come to know in the course of our lives also populate our imaginations. What we have been and who was with us from the beginning still dwell within our innermost thoughts and affect what we are ready to find in the world about us. What we have come to be and who we have come to be with represent changes in our everyday living and suggest the kinds of change we are ready or are not ready to experience. What we know and can know, what we find moral and can find moral are dimensions of this readiness for life.

The capacity for religion derives from the earliest stages of our individual development and, whether we develop an active religiosity or not, stays with us as an aspect of our very selves. By a "capacity for religion" is meant simply that the individual personally experiences reality. As with all such formulaic statements, more is being said in those few words than seems to be the case at first. Let us begin with the verb *experience*. What is being spoken of is not knowledge about something, as if from some outside perspective. It is science that deals with that latter kind of "knowledge about" things. In scientific knowledge there are concepts that are thought to correspond to realities, and those realities are thought to be separate from the ideas in some way. Experiences are not separated from what they are experiences of; they cannot be true or false about realities in the way that scientific accounts are provable or disprovable. What experiences of reality lack in system, coherence, and communicability, compared to scientific knowledge, they make up in a vividness of having been directly present to someone. The capacity for religion resides in this vivid presentness that is a feature of living as a person. That is why that capacity can be important even if not actualized by the individual in the past in explicitly religious conduct.

When we say that the individual personally experiences reality, we are referring to more than the factual reality of a psychological attentiveness, more than simply not being inert or asleep with respect to the world. We mean more than the kind of interest a cat, for example, may have in a sardine. We also mean more than "first hand," the latter a psychological state shared with other complex animals. To experience something personally implies being a person as much as it implies the experience of presentness. A person knows that other individuals live as centers of spontaneity and that one can elicit attention from them toward oneself. Early in life this attention from others may be sought out and experimented with incessantly. The child feels secure in the confidence that some other is ever there, nearby and concerned about how the child feels. Later on, the child may go to some lengths to maintain a to-and-fro with others in an effort to firm up their confidence - the back and forth exchanges of talk, play, and games. A whole repertory of skills for the rudiments of life with others develops through all this effort to attract attention. The child's sense of self, its sense of being a person, emerges in this to-and-fro with others.

In the to-and-fro of early life in families people develop enduring familial images that they can use symbolically in later life. When people take the familial symbols of their personal grounding of themselves in reality and apply those symbols to life in general, we speak of them having a religion. "God the Father" or "God the Mother" is a symbol for the spontaneous providence found "there" in reality. For some people, such a symbol carries meaning only at the level of a continuing personal experience of reality; they do not profess to know what the dimensions of reality related to such experiences are like. Some such people think of themselves as agnostic, but religiously so. Others take the familial images that inhabit their religiosity as metaphorical; the divine would be greater, in their view, than any attempted grasp of it. They may activate an explicit religiosity in the sense of engaging in prayer and congregational worship, but they do not take religious discourse to be the same kind of discourse as scientific accounts of natural reality. For them, apparent or merely verbal conflicts between religious and scientific statements are not a problem. They have no problem, for example, with the scientific theory of evolution. For other people still, the familial images that emerge in religious discourse are taken more literally. For them, God is really like a father or a mother (but not both). In whatever way any given person may fashion a discourse, if any, about religion, the capacity for religion is part and parcel of the personal experience that gives continuity and identity to the individual. The individual's attentiveness within which the person's life projects itself into the future is shaped by the way in which the capacity for religion has been developed. The ability to be religious thereby lends an individual character to the person's experienced environment and lends that character to the individual's grasp of the opportunities and systems of relevance within that environment.

While the capacity for religion has its antecedents far back in people's earliest personal experiences, it is not the only influence on the experiences they have of the environment. For better or worse, most people today live in a class society; the way they experience and interpret the world varies with the ways they make their way in the world of money and work. "Life styles" that correspond in a rough way with class standing add new features to people's imaginative processes. For example, the traditional working class maintains an idealized picture, if not always the reality, of a marked division of labor along gender lines, with the male role featuring a contribution of working hours at a job and the female role featuring child rearing and household preoccupations. The relative decline in real pay for working class employment over the past twenty-five years along with the attendant necessity for both husbands and wives to work outside the home has been undermining this pattern. However, that fact does not prevent working class men from defining their place in the world in terms of timed labor outside the home. Other people relate to these men in terms of that role; their adult experiences of the to-and-fro of life with others are structured by that role. They even come to know of their very selves in terms of that role. Typically their life histories, as they shape those histories as accounts in their minds, feature a period of youth marked by adolescent athleticism and friendship groups, followed by courtship, marriage, and work. The women define themselves in terms of family and home, even though there may be many other involvements. They focus on how others relate to them in terms of their family responsibilities and home activities. Typically their life histories, as they shape them in their minds, feature a youth marked by social events, followed by courtship, marriage and family. Both the male and female working class define themselves by these limited structures despite the fact that the men have family responsibilities and the women jobs. The men and women maintain distinct circles of friends. In many cases the men form their social networks around work associates who are often the same people they knew in childhood. The women form their social networks around the extended family and sometimes neighborhood associates, and these too are often people known from childhood.

The upper middle class places more emphasis on school during adolescence, especially preparing for and then attending college. This brings about a break from childhood social networks as well as a break from family patterns experienced during childhood (and hence considered "traditional"). The upper middle class men and women cultivate skills through extended stretches of education and practical training; they become "psychologically invested" in professions and callings, even though much of their working lives, in and out of the home, may be related in only a tangential way to the expertise they develop. Work, and consequently the individuals' insertion into society with its experiences of the to-and-fro with others, is defined in terms of the kinds of problem to be solved or the kinds of service to be rendered rather than in terms of time spent working. This makes it difficult to put a limit on work, resulting in a tendency for work to "engulf" the person, dominating more and more of the individual's waking hours.

For the working class male, religion may provide a moral compass, but having accomplished that early on it need not involve any continued active participation. Rather religion is something in which the working class women involve themselves as part of the proper early life experience to be made available to the children. The same capacity for religion, with which religious activity may be associated, that the adult developed in early life is deemed appropriate for the children's early lives; by association religious activity, as opposed to the mere capacity for it, is also deemed appropriate for the children. Consequently working class women often develop a church-based social network as a result of their religious involvements that figure into their understanding of the proper way to rear their children. They and their husbands often associate "family values" (proper role models for children) with the church.

For the upper middle class, religious involvement is less related to the traditional gender division of labor. With their extended adolescence spent in educational settings, upper middle class men and women often come to interpret religious symbols quite metaphorically; consequently their religiosity is less cognitively accessible to the children; consequently that religiosity may become more or less detached from child rearing concerns. Moreover, the college experience often results in spouses meeting each other in college and university settings, with the result of many couples in the upper middle class being approximately the same age.   They often have equal educational and financial attainments and assume child rearing responsibilities on a more equal basis.   For them the world of work is experienced as an encroachment on family life as well as an opportunity to develop a public persona.   For both men and women the struggle is to balance work and family, and the "crowded" life space they come to inhabit as a result may leave little time and energy for religious involvements.   In those instances where religious involvements do develop - or simply persist from the time of childhood - the church setting serves as a retreat from the work world.   A church based social network may be cultivated as a counter society of sorts, free of the politics and pressures of the work place.   This is sometimes symbolized by the way the upper middle class church attender resists dressing in business attire when attending services.

Reaching "older age" brings with it an undoing of much that has been accomplished by the individual after the time of childhood. Retirement may not be experienced as a crisis, but the working class male is separated from the social network of the workplace.   Even if contacts are maintained in other settings with the same set of people, one's friends, known since childhood, also reach older age at about the same time and begin to take ill and die.   The children leave home, oftentimes going to school to avail themselves of opportunities their parents did not have.   Again, this is not necessarily experienced as something negative or as a crisis, but the working class female loses an idealized role when this happens.   She is no longer shaping the home lives of children.   The two spouses at least have each other, and there can be a rewarding circumstance of a second flowering of a marriage. What happens, however, when one of the spouses dies, leaving the other as a widow or widower?   The sense of personhood has been developed in a to-and-fro with special other people, and the typical events of later life cut the individual off from that important experience.

For the upper middle class individual as well, retirement and the children leaving home are serious events.   Both may be experienced with a great deal of relief, easing the competing commitments of work and family.   Contacts with any social networks from the work places may be cut off more sharply than is the case with the working class since there is less of an overlap with childhood friendship groups; moreover, because the smaller family sizes characteristic of the upper middle classes often result in smaller extended families, there is usually less of a family based social network. Again, the spouses at least have each other, and again this can be a rewarding circumstance of a second flowering of marriages, but this makes the inevitable death of one of the spouses all the more of a crisis. Upon attaining older age, the upper middle class is as vulnerable to losing the to-and-fro experiences that support the sense of self as is the working class.

What we have sketched above is greatly simplified. For example, there are more than two classes in America; some people are poor, some wealthy enough not to need to work for a living, and many experiencing aspects of both the working and upper middle class patterns. In fact, many people do not fit neatly into either a working class or an upper middle class pattern. Sometimes working class people maintain extended cultural pursuits in an upper middle class manner; these are sometimes religious in nature, and they occasion the formation of social networks that are not affected by retirement or by children leaving home. Sometimes members of the upper middle class adhere to a highly conventional family pattern with a traditional division of labor along gender lines. Nevertheless, it remains generally true that in older age conditions may represent an undermining of much that people consider to be important in their lives and important about themselves. The working class men have at best a childhood religiosity with which to face this attack on their sense of self. The working class women have more of a community, partly based in the church, with which to face a similar attack. The upper middle class men and women have much less frequently such a supportive community, but when they have one it may be church-based.

In the next chapter we will give an account of the kinds of stressful problems older people encounter and the effects the problems have on their quality of life. In the chapter after that, we will see what role religion can play in buffering the effects of such problems on older people's subjective well-being. The presentation will use statistical information that seems to focus on one kind of problem at a time - e.g., medical difficulties and financial worries. Throughout the presentation it is necessary to remember that in every instance it is a whole person who is facing a difficulty, a person who is bringing a lifetime of experience and personal resources to a problematic experience. The person's capacity for religion helps shape the grasp of problems and the resources available for meeting them. No problem is experienced in isolation from the other dimensions of the person's life, the religious dimension included.

Ch. 3 Problems in Later Years

Problems

We all know what problems are. We have all experienced them and can point to a number of them. If we have had to deal with a particularly serious problem at some point in our lives, we may think of ourselves as having been made a better person by it, a person able to empathize with others more readily and able to stand up better under adversity. We speak of such experiences with problems as "building character." People who never seem to have had any problems might strike us as being heartless and unable to recognize the difficulties that other people face. This informal knowledge that we have amounts to a folk psychology of sorts in which the experience of serious problems plays an important part. This folk psychology serves as a summary, consisting of adages and impressions, that provides a synopsis of our own and others' accumulated crises and painful experiences. The substance that lies behind the few adages and impressions, however, consists of many details.

One way to speak about problems is to point to objective conditions that "are" the problem. Pointing to such realities is a good enough approach so far as it goes, and one would certainly not recommend recognizing as problems experiences to which no such realities correspond. However, there is much more to a problem than an external condition that we can make an object of our consideration. Many people, for example, turn to work in order to "take their minds off" of problems. The condition that "is" the problem is not changed by working at something else, but the individuals who turn to work are refusing to allow their problems to dominate their life space. In an individual's work, especially work that requires close attention, the individual is finding a way to be doing something despite the problem that may lurk in the background. The individual is making a near and present activity paramount in attention and relegating the problem, however important it may be on some theoretical scale of measures, to the margins. While an idle person may be left dwelling on a problem, the busy person keeps in control of the choice of which experience, out of many possible ones, will be dominant at a given moment in time.

It should become evident that there is another good way to speak about problems in addition to pointing to objective circumstances that comprise "the problem." We can speak about "allowing a circumstance to become a problem." Not allowing that to happen is not to deny the reality of an external circumstance that may pose difficulties or dangers but to keep the circumstance from "getting the best of us." For present purposes, we want to look at problems as both the objective circumstances and the mental state of experiencing those circumstances as pressing and paramount. This is because we are interested in what is sometimes called *well-being* and at other times called *quality of life*. While the objective problematic circumstances cannot be banished from the world of reality through magic of some kind, it remains important to maintain in some way a general sense of well-being or a generally good quality of life despite difficulties. How one responds to the objective circumstances becomes as important a dimension of a problem as the objective circumstances themselves.

In the present chapter we are interested in the occurrence in older people's lives of seriously negative experiences. In Chapter 1 we have already reviewed some of the objective circumstances that often prove to be difficult. We mentioned medical problems and the difficulties of going about the routines of daily living that stem from the medical problems or from feebleness. We also mentioned financial difficulties. We can add the stresses associated with retiring, new residential arrangements, loss of loved ones, and loneliness. Here we want to look at these various kinds of problem again, but in the course of our review we want to add considerations of how older people in fact respond to them, how they might find them to be seriously negative experiences.

This takes us to the question of symptoms of depression. We have already mentioned depression as a medical condition, and we have listed the symptoms that are used frequently to identify medical depression. Depression involves an awareness of objective problems, though it is more than a simple awareness of their existence. The depressed individual responds to the objective problems with the kinds of feeling and behavior that we mentioned as symptoms - feeling blue, neglecting appearance, not eating, and so forth. In medical depression the awareness of problems and the symptoms are organized in a system from which the individual has difficulty finding an exit; the system or "complex" keeps the symptoms in place over a long duration of time. While the medical condition of depression needs be included in any view of well-being or quality of life, we are interested in the "symptoms" even when they may not be organized as a medical condition. The symptoms themselves represent serious negative experiences that detract from a sense of well-being and from the quality of life.

Thus, while medical depression is a most serious kind of continuing negative experience, the symptomatic behaviors that *could* indicate medical depression are of interest in their own right. Researchers who study subjective well-being frequently use check lists of the widely recognized symptoms of depression not because they are interested in identifying medically depressed individuals but because they are concerned when people react behaviorally to sensing that they do not have a generally good quality of life.[1] The check list of symptoms of depression that was used for the "Depression Symptom Scores" that we report later on in this chapter is the CES-D scale.[2] In Chapter 1 we introduced some statistics from a 1990 Nashville study of older persons; a form of the CES-D scale was included in the interviews conducted in the course of that study. The average depression symptom score among the 729 people who answered all of the scale's items was 4.47. That number is not meaningful in itself, but it will serve as a point of comparison below. People with scores above 4.47 will be thought of as having a lesser quality of life than those with scores below that figure.

A very frequent kind of problem for older persons is medical. Medical problems range from mild nuisances, such as the reduced depth perception of many older eyes, to debilitating and life threatening conditions that either necessitate hospitalization or, at the end of life, necessitate living in hospices. Our present concern is with conditions that are more serious than mild nuisances and more long-term than "final illnesses." The interviews in the 1990 Nashville study included a long check list of non-trivial chronic conditions. These were conditions that either required hospitalization or required attention by clinical or medical specialists in order for the medical problems not to require hospitalization. "Medical Problem Scores" were derived from these check lists, with an average score of 4.08 for the 740 people who provided relevant information in the interviews. As in the case of the Depression Symptom score, the number itself is not meaningful but will serve as a point of comparison later on.

Another kind of problem frequently appearing among older persons is financial. If the difficulty amounts to a low income in a situation where the individual is provided for materially anyway, for example by their children, a low income stream may not really a be problem. Even with a very modest income, someone living in a house owned by a family member and sharing in the family meals may experience considerable comfort and independence; selecting what to do with leisure time, pursuing hobbies and interests, and being able to make occasional visits and trips is possible in such circumstances. We observed in Chapter 1 that it is older people living alone who often faced financial difficulties. To focus on financial *problems*, we are interested in whether given older people believe they have reason to worry about money. In the 1990 Nashville study the interviews contained a question that asked whether financial concerns caused the individuals stress. We developed a "Financial Stress Score" on the basis of the question; the 727 interviewees who provided useful answers to the question averaged 1.43 on the Financial Stress Score. Again, the number itself carries no meaning but will be used below for purposes of comparison.

There is a considerable social scientific literature about older persons' stressful life events. The thought is that events that cause rather thorough going changes in a person's life are stressful because they alter the nature of one's sense of self: who one is, who one has become comfortable being, how one is regarded in the eyes of others, and whom one associates with and identifies with. Events such as retirements and relocating to a new residence might be stressful in this way. People of all ages look even toward happy events with some trepidation - events such as graduations and weddings. Events that cause such thorough going changes and are unhappy as well are even more threatening. For older people, the death of spouses, other family members, and friends are frequently troubling events. In the 1990

Nashville study there were a number of questions asking about such events happening to the interviewees in the previous twelve months; we summed the various events into totals for each interviewee. On average, however, the respondents experienced only 0.89 such events; so in the analyses that we will present below we will compare those who have had with those who have not had one or more of the listed stressful life events to report in the previous twelve months.

Being alone most of the time can also be a serious problem. Some people are more social by nature than others and find being alone difficult while some people are more "self-contained." So being alone is not itself always a problem, depending on the nature of the person. What we have in mind is being alone when one would want someone to be nearby and interested. Company and the concern that might be expressed by others are particularly important when the individual is facing some difficulty. Being alone can make a medical problem or a financial worry doubly troubling. Having company in the face of trial is a little like work; it keeps one from dwelling on a difficulty in a morbid sort of way. How much company and how explicitly concern needs be shown is what may vary from one person to another. In the 1990 Nashville study interviewees were asked a number of questions about how much support they *thought* they received from others. We call the resultant score the "Perceived Social Support Score"; it averaged 1.43 among the 727 people who provided usable answers to all of the relevant items. Again, the average, or "mean score," will be used for comparative purposes below.

Problems and Depression Symptom Scores

As we observed above, depression symptoms need not be organized into a system to be negative experiences; they need not be tantamount to medical depression to affect the quality of life negatively. These "symptoms" are responses to objective problems, and as responses that are unhappy they are sensed as being the opposite of well-being. The present question is, How much do the different kinds of objective problem occasion these symptoms? One way to find out is to divide the interviewees in the Husaini 1990 Nashville study into separate groups - those having higher than average scores for some problem and those having lower than average scores for the problem - and then comparing the average Depression Symptom Scores for the two resultant groups.[3] Thus, for example, we can look at the "mean" of the Depression Symptom Scores for those with more than average chronic medical problems and find out whether they are higher or lower than the "mean" of the Depression Symptom Scores for those with fewer than average chronic medical problems.

Medical problems can occasion negative experiences by causing pain, by reducing the physical energy available for activities, by requiring that the individual be confined to a limited space, by making the individual dependent on others for various daily activities, by necessitating the use of medications that have noxious or disabling side effects, and by requiring the expenditures of sums of money that one can ill afford to spend, for items not covered by Medicare or supplemental medical insurance. It would certainly be no surprise to find that people with more than an average number of chronic medical problems, as indicated by a check list, would also have higher than average Depression Symptom Scores. We find in Table 3.1 that this was in fact the case among the interviewees (all of them older persons) in the Husaini 1990 Nashville study. Medical difficulties were not only problems in the obvious sense of being objectively unwanted conditions but also constituted a problem in the sense of eliciting symptoms that are often associated with depression.

Table 3.1: Depression Symptom Scale Means By Medical Problems

Medical Problems	Depression Symptom Scale Means	(N)
More than average	5.97*	(351 respondents)
Less than average	3.07	(378 respondents)

*Statistically significant at .01 level.
Source: Baqar A. Husaini

A second kind of problem that we have described is financial. In a simple sense, a financial problem is not having *enough* money. The reality is more complex than that, of course, because enough is an elastic word. Someone who owns and maintains a house, for example, needs money for upkeep, and someone who rents an apartment needs to pay the rent; however, someone who lives with others - e.g., members of the family - may need much less money, but need "enough" to engage in various activities independently. Someone whose income stream needs to meet the needs of two or more people needs more income than someone whose income meets the need of only themselves, but those who live alone often have a smaller income than those who live with others. Those who have medical problems need money for expenses that are not covered by medical insurance while those who are in good health do not need money for that.[4]

A financial problem does not bring on an immediate physiological discomfort the way a medical problem does, but it may bring on worry. That kind of worry is one of the experiences people refer to when they say that they "feel blue." The worry can be about meeting one's own material needs, about using up much of the income stream of one's family members, or about having to depend on charity or welfare after a lifetime of providing for oneself and others. Beyond worry, having less than enough money can lead one to a sense of failure. The failure may not only be the opposite of success, but may be tied up with a sense of moral failure, of having been improvident in some way. Financial success and failure is bound up with all sorts of social values in American culture, not merely with economic issues; and this fact affects people even in cases where there may be good reasons for them not to feel responsible for a financial difficulty. Consequently we would not be surprised to find that interviewees in the Husaini 1990 Nashville study who scored above average on the financial Stress Scale score also scored above average on the Depression Symptom Scale; this was in fact how it turned out (see Table 3.2).

Table 3.2: Depression Symptom Scale Means By Financial Stress

Financial Stress	Depression Symptom Scale Means	(N)
Above average score	6.66*	(223 respondents)
Less than average score	3.51	(457 respondents)

*Statistically significant at .01 level
Source: Baqar A. Husaini

Having a persistent problem such as a chronic medical condition or an insufficient stream of income is a qualitatively different kind of experience from undergoing a sudden or one-time-only negative event. A stressful event may catch attention and be easily pointed out; it is socially easier to make mention of tragedies that reach "closure" and become a thing of the past. To dwell on a persisting problem is to "complain" and is therefore regarded differently in social settings.   This leaves it open whether stressful events will be accompanied by the depression symptoms in the way that chronic medical conditions and financial stress seem to be. This is not to minimize the seriousness of such events as relocating to a new residential situation or, especially, loss of a spouse, but there is no guarantee that the nature of the personal impact is the same as for the persisting problems. When we divided the interviewees from the Husaini 1990 study into two groups - those with one or more stressful life events in the previous twelve months and those with none - and compared the corresponding mean scores on the Depression Symptom Scale, there was in fact not much difference between the two groups' means (see Table 3.3). The dramatic events to which we can readily point do not necessarily affect the subjective well-being of the individual (as we are conceiving of it in the present discussion).[5]

Table 3.3: Depression Symptom Scale Means By Stressful Life Events

Stressful Life Events	Depression Symptom Scale Means (N)
1 or more in past 12 months	4.79 (422 respondents)
None in past 12 months	4.03 (307 respondents)

Source: Baqar A. Husaini

One kind of persistent problem that people may face is an absence of social support. This may be in part a matter of isolation, of being alone. However, it is not simply a question of being physically proximate or not physically proximate to other people. Being near people who do not seem to take an interest in oneself is a negative rather than gratifying experience. On the other hand, being some distance from others or living alone but hearing from them often by letter or telephone and knowing that one can rely on them when help may be needed (e.g., in times of illness) is not really a problem. In order to focus on social support as a rewarding circumstance and on its opposite as a problem, interviewees were asked a number of questions in the Husaini 1990 Nashville study that were designed to see how much social support the interviewees believed themselves to enjoy. When comparing the Depression Symptom Scale score means of interviewees who had more and those who had less perceived social support, it can indeed be found that those with less perceived social support had higher Depression Symptom Scale scores (see Table 3.4).

Table 3.4: Depression Symptom Scale Means By Perceived Social Support Scores

Perceived Social Support Scores	Depression Symptom Scale Means	(N)
Higher than average	3.40	(571 respondents)
Lower than average	8.32*	(158 respondents)

*Statistically significant at .01 level
Source: Baqar A. Husaini

Perceived social support appears to be such an important factor in people's subjective well-being that it needs to be taken into consideration even when looking at the other factors. For example, while medical problems may occasion responses that are symptomatic of depression, it may also be the case that a medical problem may stir family and friends up to provide support of various kinds - telephone calls, visits, offers of practical help, actual help with daily living activities. The individual with the medical problem may be gratified by such support even while suffering some discomfort from the medical condition itself. This can clearly happen with a short-term medical crisis, though whether it is likely to happen with a chronic condition is an open question. Because of such possibilities, it is interesting to see whether the experience of problems actually seemed to occasion higher scores on the Perceived Social Support Scale (see Table 3.5). As it turns out in the Husaini 1990 Nashville study, the two long-term problems - the chronicle medical problems and financial stress - were not associated with the Perceived Social Support Score means in any statistically significant way, but having one or more stressful life events in the previous twelve months was associated with higher perceived social support scores. The importance of perceived social support will affect our analysis of the role of religion in subjective well-being in the next chapter.

Table 3.5: Perceived Social Support Scale Means By Problems

Problem	Perceived Social Support Scale Means (N)	
Chronic medical problem		
More than average	21.05	(355 respondents)
Less than average	21.42	(385 respondents)
Financial stress		
Higher than average	21.22	(226 respondents)
Lower than average	21.33	(501 respondents)
Stressful events in previous 12 months		
One or more	21.66*	(423 respondents)
None in previous 12 months	20.69	(317 respondents)

*Statistically significant at .01 level
Source: Baqar A. Husaini

Conclusion

When we think of problems as not merely difficult situations that people face but also as people being troubled by the difficulties, we can begin to see the connection between problems and people's subjective well-being. Behavioral responses to problems include the "symptoms" that may be indicative of medical depression, if those symptoms are organized into a system from which it is difficult for a person to exit. How a person conceives of a problem and how a person is prone to respond to difficulties can be seen in this context as a factor in the person's well-being or quality of life. In the next chapter we demonstrate that religion can be an important element in affecting the subjective well-being of the older person who faces typical problems. Religion can influence how a person conceives of a difficulty, how the person responds to difficulties once they are perceived, and what social network is available to provide social support for the individual in the face of problems.

Notes

     1. In fact, such check lists do not work well as screens for medical depression.

     2. Center for Epidemiologic Studies - Depression Scale. See L. Radloff, "The CES-D scale: A self-report depression scale for research in the general population," *Applied Psychological Measurement 1* (1977): 385-401.

     3. Readers with some statistical background should refer to Appendix One for a regression analysis. The presentation that follows below in the present chapter is limited to comparisons of mean scores in tables. For a discussion based on the regression analysis, see B.A. Husaini, A.J. Blasi, and O. Miller, "Religion Moderating Depression Among the Elderly: Race Differences in the American South," forthcoming in the *International Journal of Aging and Human Development.*

     4. Statistically sophisticated readers may be concerned that the "effects" of medical problems on depression symptom scores might be confounded with the "effects" of financial worries. Please refer to Appendix One, where "independent" effects are demonstrated.

     5. In the regression analysis (see Appendix One) we combined the sum of stressful life events with the financial stress scores, thereby creating a "Social Stress" score. The stressful life events indicator slightly enhanced the predictive power of the financial stress indicator, using the depression symptom scale (CES-D) as the dependent variable.

Ch. 4 Religion as a Resource

Having reviewed some of the significant problems that older people typically encounter in our society, we want to examine religion as a resource that may help them face the problems. Considering religion as that kind of resource is not to say that religious people invariably use it for facing problems or that it invariably has the effect of bettering their subjective well-being in the face of problems, but only that it can be used in that way or have that effect. If we can demonstrate, as we hope to do in later sections of this chapter, that some religiously active people are subjectively better off than some less religiously active people, we will have given some support to the idea that religion can be a resource. First we need to spell out why it might be that religion can be a resource in the face of problems.

Religious Perspective

A person's religion involves an outlook on the world. Typically, that outlook provides a framework or context into which the religious person might place specific events and experiences. There might be a hierarchy of values in which comfort and convenience do not receive much priority. There might be a moral order in which rendering and receiving service is highly valued. There might be a focus on prayer, wherein the presence of the divine in the consciousness of the individual takes precedence over feelings and physical conditions. There may be an afterlife that serves as the ultimate evaluation and commentary on a life in this world. Because any one religious tradition or denomination may be marked by a variety of differing religious outlooks, it would be an error for us to look for more or less monolithic depictions of the world that would be held by the adherents of any one religion. Rather, we need to be interested in how an individual person might look upon the world, and we need to be interested in whether or not a person can have a better quality of life because of a personal religious perspective.

When a perspective, be it religious or not, provides a context for other experiences and points of knowledge rather than the other experiences and points of knowledge serving as a context for it, when a perspective occasions insights into other aspects of life with the latter providing applications for the perspective rather than insights into it, we speak of it as an *ultimate concern*; it provides the individual person with an ultimate reality upon which to focus or an ultimate meaning that affects the meanings of everything else.[1] Religions usually present their adherents with such an ultimate concern, leaving it up to the believer to make that concern really ultimate in practice. An ultimate concern can engage the individual's attention. The pursuit of it is similar to working. It can distract the individual in both a good and a bad sense - good insofar as people do not dwell on their problems pointlessly and morbidly, bad insofar as they might accept whatever happens fatalistically and not help themselves when they can in fact do so. It is the potential of religion as a perspective that can "distract" in the good sense of that term that is of interest here. As an ultimate perspective, a religion can distract the individual from a problem that worry cannot help and thereby keep the problem from becoming a morbid fixation.

A religion can also provide people with a framework of priorities that lead beyond selfish or self-centered concerns. The philanthropic or service dimension in many religious traditions may inspire people to undertake works on altruistic grounds. Such charitable works may or may not satisfy the needs that can be found in the world; indeed, needs are often so large-scale that only governments of major nations together with philanthropic foundations can produce a noticeable impact. Nevertheless altruistic inspirations in people who control neither large governments nor large charitable foundations can lead to small scale good effects and serve to lead people to work at rewarding tasks rather than dwell on their own problems. The works in question may be charitable (e.g., visiting the ill, running soup kitchens) or specifically religious (e.g., collecting and distributing religious literature, leading religious discussions, singing in a choir) or even political (e.g., participating in a campaign on behalf of some ethical stand).

One important aspect of a religious perspective may consist of a sympathetic divine personage. In Christian tradition, for example, there is the figure of a sympathetic divine savior who endured suffering as a human in the course of reaching out to humans. When whatever befalls the individual is thought to be of interest to an ultimate personage, the individual is likely to be comforted. One's past experiences of social support from others can be retrieved from memory and associated with the divine personage; this is what may occur in prayer. When individuals have had the opportunity to become sophisticated in prayer, prayer in the face of problems ceases to be an effort to compel the divine to give them what they cannot obtain for themselves and begins to become a cultivation of a relationship between those who pray and the deity who provides for what is ultimately important. Prayer itself becomes the focus, rather than some result to be obtained by prayer.[2] The focus on a sympathetic savior figure rather than what a deity might give when prayed to would appear to help prayer enhance subjective well-being rather than have it contribute to a fixation on problems.

For many people religion can be a long-term interest. We know rather intuitively that people who have interests are better off subjectively than people who are not interested in anything. Why this is so calls for some consideration. Having a long-term interest entails a personal history of doing something. It is not a matter of performing discrete acts that are trivial in themselves and deservedly forgotten but of working at one "thing." Numerous actions contribute to that one thing. One may collect objects, keep a scrap book, read up on a subject, go to conventions. Consequently one comes to know oneself as someone active in some "field" or concern. A particular course of activity is known as one's own; it has become internalized. One's own activity with respect to the interest populates one's imagination. Consequently, even if one must be less active because of illness or some other limitation, one may still associate the active dimension in one's imagination with oneself. In the case of religion, someone who has been active in religion over a long term may have a self-knowledge as an active individual. This can lend one a sense of personal control or personal mastery that may contribute toward the person's subjective well-being.[3]

Of course, not all religion is the same. It is frequently useful to distinguish private from public religious activity. Private religious activity includes praying by oneself, reading the Bible or other religious literature, thinking about religious subjects, listening to religious music, and any other activity that is in some way religious and is done alone. Public religious activity includes attendance at and especially participating in congregational worship services, as well as in various group activities that may be conducted under church auspices. Some religious activities fall between the public and private sides of religion; they may occur in small group settings. The difference between private and public religion is important because some of the problems that older people typically face place limits on public religious activity, while the disengagement from occupational roles so characteristic of later life actually allows more time for private religious activity. Religion as a resource for facing problems is itself going to be affected by some of those problems and is going to be maintained in varying ways.

The Church Community

Congregations and small groups within congregations comprise an important aspect of many major religions, especially in the Western traditions. Social scientists sometimes distinguish between magic, which addresses the instrumental needs of individuals, and religion, which is an inherently social supernaturalism. Magic can even be used against someone within one's community, while religion would be an expression of a community.[4] These uses of the terms magic and religion have not found universal acceptance among scholars because belief systems that are communally shared, and hence religious, are sometimes used "magically" for individual instrumental purposes and some clearly non-instrumental supernaturalist orientations are peculiar to one or two persons rather than communal in nature. Despite the differences over terminology, there is general agreement that much religion is communal. In the modern industrial nations the community which serves as the vehicle for a religious expression is frequently the local congregation.

By bringing congregations into existence and giving them their reason for continuing through time, religion serves as a social resource as well as an individual one. Congregations bring people together who might otherwise never meet each other, and consequently friendship networks often develop among congregation members. The number of people individuals may know may be increased by virtue of membership in church congregations. The very maintenance of these friendship networks can result in people looking to others rather than dwelling on one or more problems that they may themselves have. The interest that congregation members may take in one another's welfare may lead naturally to expressions of concern about medical problems, for example, and thereby enhance the individual's perception of mattering to others. Moreover it is common in congregations for members to pray for one another - an activity that itself expresses interest and concern.

A congregation's public religion, its collective worship services, is an obvious occasion of people coming to meet one another, but it is in small group activities that they really come to know one another. The worship services themselves afford little opportunity for conversation and company. However, choir practices, study groups, charitable works and the like bring people with like interests together into natural friendship groups. They also serve as the occasion for activities, which give individuals the experience of "making a difference," of being efficacious. These experiences can be expected to give the individuals a sense of "personal control." Personal control has been found to be associated with subjective well-being.

The church community as a social resource should not be thought of in isolation from religion as an ultimate perspective. Religious beliefs, precisely because they refer to ultimate realities, depend upon faith rather than demonstration. Faith is an inherently precarious state of mind that depends upon companions who believe in the same tradition and base their actions on the same set of values and meanings. The congregational faith community and its resident intellectuals provide a social support for the religious perspective, a social support that sociologists call a *plausibility structure*.[5] Not only do one's fellow members articulate rationales in support of the precarious perspective of one's religion, but to remain a member in good standing one wants to share in their cognitive perspective. In supporting a given religious perspective in this way, the congregational community also supports the potential for that perspective to serve as a resource for subjective well-being.

Potential Effects

It would be misleading to limit one's view of the role of religion in mitigating the effects of stress to what happens once stressful events occur or after stressful conditions begin. Before a difficulty develops, a religious perspective that cognitively places a difficulty within a larger system of meanings and priorities can prevent that difficulty from being interpreted as a major problem. An active local faith community can prevent loneliness from occurring. The congregation-based social network can also provide for minor instrumental needs such as transportation and home repairs, so that minor difficulties do not become major ones. Older people of limited means living in rough neighborhoods especially face something like a physicians' appointment as a threatening situation if it requires standing outside, perhaps in cold weather, waiting for a bus, vulnerable before anyone who may happen to be in the vicinity. Friendly transportation provided by a friend from the church will not only avoid such an anxiety-producing situation but make it more likely that the individual will make physicians' appointments when appropriate in the first place.

Once stressful events do occur or stressful conditions do develop, how much of a problem they are to the individual is an important factor, as we saw in Chapter 3. If a person places less emphasis on economic concerns and more emphasis on spiritual ones, financial difficulties should have lessened effects. Perhaps more importantly, the conditions associated with advanced age that disrupt occupational and family roles may not disrupt the religious ones. If who one is in the social world is related to one's job, if the people one knows are to a great extent the people one knows from the work place, retirement has the effect of depriving one of part of one's self. If who one is in the social world is related to providing for and rearing children or to "being there" for a spouse, living alone as a widow or widower is to live similarly deprived of part of one's self. If, however, a major part of one's life consists of performing a particular service in the local church congregation, if one knows oneself at least in part as an active religious agent, that part of one's self can be maintained well into old age. In fact, prior to being "very old" one's religious activity with others may increase rather than decrease. Such activity can help a person maintain a sense of making a difference in the world and of being in control of things. Contrary to some stereotypes, religious activity need not be associated with fatalism but may instead engender a sense of personal control.

There is yet another way that religion can support a person's subjective well-being. Even after a difficulty has developed and has become a problem that brings on some of the symptoms of depression, the church congregation and its ministers to older persons can help the individual respond to the depression symptoms intelligently. Many clergy and many lay ministers to older persons have professional training in counseling. They may not have enough training to deal in any professional way with conditions that may require pharmacological treatment or "talk therapy," but they can recognize who may need that kind of attention and refer the individual to a trustworthy specialist. Many people may lack insight into their own conditions and may be apprehensive about the very idea of stresses affecting them. They may not distinguish between how they cope physically and psychologically with problems on the one hand and their intelligence and adequacy as individuals on the other. Someone who can help them clarify such issues can in the process help them get the professional attention they need before a situation becomes a crisis.[6]

Demonstrating Effects

Actually demonstrating any effects of religion on the subjective well-being of older persons is not easy. Religious involvement itself takes many different forms. The typical questionnaire item asking about the frequency with which someone attends religious services misses the difference between someone who arrives early and helps lead a Sunday school session before the main service and someone who merely arrives and listens. With respect to older persons, it misses the difference between someone who attends seldom because of disinterest and someone who attends seldom because of health problems. Similarly, asking about participation in church activities apart from worship overlooks the degree of involvement, as opposed to frequency of showing up, and fails to consider the consequences of bad health. Consequently, when a scale of Public Religiosity[7] was formed out of two questions from the Husaini 1990 Nashville study of older people - one question asking about frequency of worship service attendance and the other asking about participation in other church activities - no particular relationship could be found between the scale and either Perceived Social Support or the Depression Symptom Scale (see Table 4.1). Both scale means are virtually the same for those scoring higher than average and lower than average on the public religious involvement scores.

Table 4.1: Public Religion by Perceived Social Support and Depression Symptoms

	Perceived Social Support	Depression Symptoms
Public Religion Score		
Higher than average	21.1(445 respondents)	4.55 (439 respondents)
Lower than average	21.6(291 respondents)	4.38 (287 respondents)

Source: Baqar A. Husaini

Table 4.1 presents something of a non-finding, but let's suppose there are other relevant factors at work. What if medical problems lead African Americans to rely more heavily than otherwise on help from family and friends while similar medical problems lead white Americans to experience greater isolation and distance from family and friends? It could be a matter of African Americans' social network centering more in one geographical locality than happens on average with white Americans. If the whites who have medical problems are the ones who cannot attend church, those of them who do attend would be the ones with higher Perceived Social Support Scores. It becomes impossible to account for all relevant factors when setting up a table such as Table 4.1, but there are more sophisticated statistical ways to conduct analyses where all such factors are figured into an analysis of "effects." Public religion does turn out to be related to Perceived Social Support scores on average for whites, but not for African American older persons; those whites who attended church worship services and other church activities more perceived more social support. Conversely, the Medical Problem Scores were related to Perceived Social Support scores on average for African Americans, but not for whites; those African American older persons who had more medical problems perceived that they enjoyed more social support.[8] One wonders whether a more sophisticated indicator of public religious involvement, especially one that reveals whether the individual actively participates in some small group that does something active in the church and thereby becomes a small social network in its own right, would show a more obvious relationship between public religious involvement and both Perceived Social Support and Depression Symptom Scores. We know, however, that Perceived Social Support is inversely related to Depression Symptom Scores - the more perceived support the fewer depression symptoms. If a more sophisticated indicator of public religious involvement could reveal some relationship between congregational small group involvement and perceived social support, the local church might be shown to be a very important element in older people's subjective well-being. The information we have on hand at the moment demonstrates this to be the case only for whites, and even then only after statistical "controls."

The Husaini 1990 study of older people in Nashville also included a number of interview questions that asked about private religious activities. The questions asked how often within the previous year the respondents shared with another church member the problems and joys of trying to live a life of faith in God, how often they read the Bible or other religious material, how often they sought guidance from statements and publications by the Church and the Bible when facing social problems and issues, how much they watched television evangelicals, how often they listened to gospel music, and how much they prayed. The responses to these questions were summed up as Private Religiosity Scores. This is by no means a perfect indicator of private religiosity because "how often" does not necessarily indicate "how important" an activity might be in someone's consciousness, but it is what we can put together as a score on the basis of the questions asked back in 1990.

In contrast to the hardly visible effects of public religious involvement, private religiosity has obvious relationships with both Perceived Social Support and Depression Symptom Scores (see Tables 4.2 and 4.3).[9] For the total sample of respondents as well as for both of the racial categories, those with higher than average Private Religiosity Scores had significantly higher mean scores on the Perceived Social Support scale. Conceivably this could be either because social networks that develop in the church community help maintain higher levels of both social support and private religiosity, or

Table 4.2: Perceived Social Support and Private Religiosity

Perceived Social Support Means (N)

Private Religiosity	Total Sample	African America	White
More than average	21.92* (416)	22.63* (130)	21.47* (232)
Less than average	20.28 (152)	21.37 (78)	20.41 (128)

*Figure is greater at .05 level of significance
Source: Baqar A. Husaini

it could be because private religiosity is in some way related to interpreting and appreciating the actions of others around oneself as supportive. It could also be the case that privately religious individuals have associates who are supportive. In part by working through Perceived Social Support[10] and in part directly, private religiosity appears to work against depression symptoms (see Table 4.3).

Table 4.3: Depression Symptoms and Private Religiosity

Private Religiosity	Depression Symptoms (N)	
More than average	3.92	(412 respondents)
Less than average	5.41*	(150 respondents)

*Figure greater at .05 level of significance
Source: Baqar A. Husaini

Conclusion

Conceptually we have good reason to expect public religious involvement to prevent some problems that frequently afflict older people by occasioning the formation of small social groups within local congregations and by supporting private religiosity. This does not mean that the usual measure of public religious involvement - frequency of worship service attendance or attendance at other church activities - can be used as a straightforward indicator of church-based social support or as a predictor of beneficial outcomes on such measures as depression symptom scales. Some of the medical problems that older people face limit attendance at events of any kind.

Moreover, attendance at events does not measure with any accuracy the formation of social networks within the congregation. It is the latter that would appear to be most critical to the subjective well-being of congregation members. After problems emerge in people's lives, participating in the life of a congregation might make it more likely that a pastor or minister to older persons will be in contact with a person and provide clarification or referrals for purposes of counseling or treatment.

How and how much public religious involvement supports private religiosity is an open question. Public religious involvement might stimulate religious interest, but people who involve themselves in activities of a practical kind, such as helping the worship service along by singing in the choir or visiting the sick, are not necessarily the people who are likely to cultivate a spiritual interiority or to find prayer an intrinsically satisfying endeavor. The possible strength of public religious involvement in the relative absence of private devotionalism and vice-versa are patterns that can occur not only among individuals but subcultures as well. Some cultural traditions, varying by denomination or by ethnicity, may be more works-oriented and others prayer-oriented. Some may seek to establish connections between public and private domains of life.

Private religiosity seems to be related to people's perception that they enjoy social support; by virtue of that and through direct effects private religiosity also seems to moderate the occurrence of the symptoms of depression. Private religiosity may direct the individual's attention to questions beyond individual problems, may establish a scale of values in which individual difficulties are seen as relatively unimportant, or may help the person see and appreciate the support to be found from others. It might even be the case that private religiosity is intrinsically rewarding and leaves the individual in a relatively happy state, even before any difficulty has had a chance to become a major problem.

In these many ways, religion - both public involvement and private devotionalism - appears to have a relevance for the quality of life of the older person. However, people are not always willing to embrace religion enthusiastically in the modern world. The extra-religious cultural baggage that specific religious traditions often bring with them may put some people off. Practical and scientifically oriented people may not be able to accept the "magical" aspects of some religious embodiments - seemingly forcing cures from God, for example, or rejecting the plausible theory of evolution. For other people, the reverse is a problem; a religion that does not produce miracles or that accepts evolution has "sold out." Other people may reject the "strictness" of the religions they know; rules against jewelry, dance, or liquor may become barriers to involvement in religion. For other people yet, it is the absence of a strict scheme of rules that is a problem. Others may associate religion with childhood rather than adulthood; it may seem to be principally a way of teaching children right from wrong. Other people yet associate religion with a more intellectual tradition that was not quite accessible to them in their childhoods. For most people in modern societies, religion is a voluntary activity associated with Sunday morning; it does not seem to have any direct bearing on the rest of the week.

Different denominational traditions vary greatly in the degree to which such barriers are present. For people who happened to belong to one church, or for that matter to no church, because of the accidental circumstances of their childhood, it may make sense to investigate different denominations and even different congregations within a denomination. If the church of one's childhood is not "right" for one's adulthood, some exploration is in order. Because many people are engulfed in work and family roles in their young adulthood, their religious involvement may be minimal until older adulthood. Then when they are ready for a greater religious involvement and may indeed benefit greatly from it, the one religion they know from childhood may be one over which they are greatly ambivalent. Such feelings of ambivalence are themselves real and are based on real life experiences. Rather than allowing them to dominate one's life, it is better to examine what ambivalence over religion there may be. Chapter 5 explores the features of our modern world that are often responsible for ambivalence over religion.

Notes

1. Tibor Horvath, "Foreword," *Ultimate Reality and Meaning 1:1* (1978): 1-8, presents a program statement for a survey of philosophical, religious, aesthetic, natural scientific, social scientific, and cultural ultimate perspectives. The masthead of the journal presents this formulation of ultimate reality and meaning: "that to which the human mind reduces and relates

everything and...does not reduce and relate to anything else" or "world views in the light of which" one "understands" or that "for which someone would sacrifice everything and...not lose for anything."

2. In a parallel concern in the psychology of religion, an extrinsic religious interest is frequently contrasted to an intrinsic one, religion as important for what someone hopes to obtain from it versus religion as important in itself. For a more precise and more extensive discussion, see M.J. Meadow and R.D. Kahoe, *Psychology of Religion. Religion in Individual Lives* (New York: Harper & Row, 1984), pp. 286-299.

3. The importance of activity as a theme was noted by R.L. Rubinstein, *Singular Paths: Old Men Living Alone* (New York: Columbia University Press, 1986), pp. 64, 75, 84-86.

4. A famous discussion of this distinction between religion and magic is found in B. Malinowski, "Magic, Science and Religion," in Malinowski, *Magic, Science and Religion and Other Essays* (Garden City: Doubleday & Company, 1954), pp. 17-92.

5. On plausibility structures, see Peter L. Berger, *The Sacred Canopy. Elements of a Sociological Theory of Religion* (Garden City, N.Y.: Doubleday and Company, 1967), pp. 45ff.

6. See Harold G. Koenig and Andrew J. Weaver, *Counseling Troubled Older Adults. A Handbook for Pastors and Religious Caregivers* (Nashville: Abingdon, 1997), pp. 15-32.

7. The mean score for the Public Religion indicator was 7.88 for the 754 respondents. This figure has no intrinsic meaning, but it served as the cut-off point between "above" and "below" average scores in Table 4.1. The mean score for the 390 African American respondents was 6.14 and for the 364 white respondents was 9.75. It should be recalled that whites have on average longer life spans than do African Americans; consequently there is likely a higher percentage of the African American respondents in the study in bad health, within a year or two of death. One should therefore not conclude that the difference in mean scores indicates a lower level of public religious involvement on the part of the African American Nashvillians in the course of their lives; in fact survey results usually indicate higher levels of public religious involvement for African Americans, compared to whites.

8. These relationships are shown statistically in the analysis presented in Appendix One at the end of the volume.

9. The Private Religiosity mean score was 5.92 for the 586 respondents who completed that part of the 1990 interviews; the mean was 6.79 for the 226 African American respondents and 5.37 for the 360 white respondents. The 5.92 figure was used in the first column of Table 4.2 and in Table 4.3 for dividing the respondents who were higher than average from those lower than average in private religiosity scores. Once statistical controls for other factors enter into the analysis, the predictive power of private religion

for Perceived Social Support among white respondents all but disappears, while a weak direct inverse relationship with Depression Symptom Scores remains. For African American respondents, private religiosity positively correlates with Perceived Social Support and, similar to the case for the white respondents, has some direct inverse relationship with Depression Symptom Scores. For details, see Appendix One at the end of the volume.

    10. We know this from the multivariate analysis presented in Appendix One.

Ch. 5 Ambivalence Over Religion

Ambivalence[1] is a condition in which people feel mixed emotions or sense mixed evaluations. In ambivalence, people have "experiences of mixed feelings, a vague and diffuse sense of being pulled in two directions...." There is the sense "...of feeling pushed or pulled, even though we have a defined and normal emotion pulling in a different direction...."[2] It would not be an adequate account of ambivalence simply to describe its psychological symptoms, however. It is not the case that people necessarily develop feelings of ambivalence because of their individual internal developmental dynamics. Ambivalence is not entirely internal;[3] rather the condition of ambivalence often reflects in a realistic fashion ambivalent situations. One part of reality pulls us one way, another part pulls us in the opposite direction.[4] Our present interest is in the situation in which religion impinges on peoples' lives in contradictory ways and is therefore experienced with mixed evaluations and mixed emotions.

If, as we have seen, religious involvements have salutary effects for the well-being of older persons, and if ambivalence accompanies those religious involvements, then the social situations that engender mixed evaluations and mixed emotions over religion can be very important factors in the ability of religion to "deliver" the desired effects. The congregation-based minister to older persons needs be aware of the ambivalence that accompanies religion in the contemporary world. Ambivalence might undermine an important cultural resource that people would otherwise have for supporting their subjective well-being in old age. It is unlikely that we can change the structural features of our society that lead people to be ambivalent about religion, and certainly we cannot remake the biographical backgrounds that led people into such ambivalence in the first place. We can, however, identify and come to understand a situation that may weaken people's ability to enjoy later life. If people can see why they feel ambivalent about something, religious involvement included, they might not allow that ambivalence to keep them from doing what they would otherwise do unhindered.

Let us begin with a simple and straightforward situation. No real life experience is simple and straightforward, but we can describe a pure case against which we can compare our own individual situations.[5] Someone may have been brought to church as a child and therefore may be able to describe themselves as "fundamentally" religious, even if they may have no history of extensive religious involvements as an adult. God may be imaged by such a person in parental terms, and other people who share such imagery might reinforce such a picture of the divine. The very idea of God would bring with it a host of parental features. God loves, provides, and disciplines in a parent-like manner. The sense of self of the child is given form on the basis of such early impressions; the child becomes conscious of itself in its exchanges with its parents. The fundamental self concept of most of us includes the experience of being the child of specific parents, and the features of parents thereby figure into the features of our selves. The features of the parents are not the features of the self, but they helped give form to the self. Thus as God loves, provides, and disciplines in the manner of a parent, "I"[6] know myself primarily as the one loved by parents, provided for by parents, and disciplined by parents. Through this connection God is tied up with who I am and how I know myself. Long ago, however, I stood up on my own two feet and left the nursery. Doing so was not an act of willful rebellion; in fact my parents led me by the hand and encouraged me to be an autonomous individual. I set out ever so tentatively into a confusing and challenging world, and soon I made my way with a certain feeling of enthusiasm. I met new people and relished the experience. I was somebody other than a child to them and to myself. In time I even became responsible for others. I surely still have a warm place in my heart of hearts for God and my first memories, but I cannot go back and be a child again.

How can this person enter into religious involvements without ambivalence complicating matters every step of the way? How can there not be reservations that need be dealt with? How especially can the person who has dropped out of any active religiosity during adolescence return without the pretense of still being the child that is no more? A conversion experience may help; an "old life" would be defined as evil and a "new life" as a gift from God. But can one really feel a regret for no longer being a child? A conversion from one religion to another may also help; the imagery used for God may differ from that used during childhood. But how does one connect this to the cherished warm place in the heart, which remains an integral part of oneself? One can educate oneself in religion, making many small connections across childhood and adolescence, and later between adolescence and early adulthood, and then between early adulthood and later adulthood; but most people are not prepared for such intellectual and emotional labor. Most have not had the luxury of time for making all these connections through the courses of their lives. The problem is endemic to adult religiosity, and it ceases to be a problem when reflected upon adequately. The difficulty is that the reflection process itself occasions feelings of ambivalence.

The Marginality of Religion and Consequences of Marginality

Social scientists have glib formulae for describing society, the comprehensive human environment that envelops our experiences. We speak of society's *structure* as the *relationships among the society's institutions*. It is easy to pass over the import of the various terms used in that formulation and thereby miss the implications of the structure of our society for the experience of religion. *Structure* in the physical world refers to resistance against changes of form. Ice cubes have structure in a way that unfrozen water sitting in ice cube trays does not. When I press on an ice cube, it will not readily lose its cube shape; when I push my finger into some water sitting in a cube space of an ice tray, it simply spills over the sides into other cube spaces. By analogy, life with others has structure. We cannot do some things without encountering resistance. That resistance may take the form of people avoiding certain situations, passing along gossip about certain courses of action, expressing disapproval, or even calling upon authorities to enforce regulations and laws.

An *institution* (by which term we do not mean "organization") is a widespread, structured aspect of collective life. The family, for example, is an institution and as such takes form and maintains its presence in the social world in particular organized entities called *families*. Similarly business is an institution that is visible to us in particular organized enterprises. Religion, of course, is also an institution, as is government.[7] When we speak of a society's structure in terms of a relationship among institutions, the suggestion is that there is resistance against changing the patterned connections and separations among various collections of organizations. Mixing family and business may engender resistance if one works for a corporation or for some other formal entity of any size. Mixing family and religion, however, may not engender resistance, unless different family members adhere to different religions.

Our society has "macro" and "micro" institutions.[8] *Macro* and *micro* are simply the Greek words for "big" and "little"; they refer to how big or a small the scope of a view or picture is. For example, we speak of microscopes having a small-scaled view or picture. Macro institutions are those that in fact are central to the big picture of the social world. Big business and big government appear to be the macro institutions of our present society.[9] The familiar micro institutions are the family, the school, and religion. If a big business fails, moves out of town, or is bought out, there will be many consequences for families, schools, and churches. Families may have to move from one city to another, perhaps even across international boundaries. Family heads may have to go into different lines of work. School systems may lose their tax base or may have to redesign their curricula to help attract a different kind of big business to their localities. Churches may lose their membership to other locations, may have to provide counseling for families that are disintegrating under financial straits or for individuals whose sense of worth is disintegrating in the experience of unemployment.

On the other hand, micro institutions seldom have such consequences for macro institutions. If a family breaks up, that has no particular importance for a corporation or government bureau. In fact, management may make it known to individuals that their family problems should not be allowed to interfere with their job performance. If a school system is ineffective, a company can simply recruit staff from out of town or can provide support for private schools. If a church undergoes a schism or because of suburbanization cannot retain its membership and must sell its building, that is of no particular importance to a big business (save a possible interest in the church real estate) or to big government. The difference between macro and micro institutions lies largely in the asymmetrical relationship between their respective organizations. The organizations of the macro institutions ("macro organizations") routinely create consequences for the organizations of the micro institutions ("micro organizations"), but the reverse situation is rare. The micro institutions, including religion, are *marginal* to the macro ones.

As a result, any given individual can only rarely escape having significant dealings with macro institutions and experiencing them as factually important, while experiencing involvements in religion and family is voluntary, episodic, and important only in terms of an idealized set of priorities. Inevitably one's sense of accomplishment, failure, and control over one's life will be worked out in the dealings with the macro institutions, not the micro ones. The experience of everyday life becomes sectored into formal involvements with powerful organizations on the one hand and informal involvements on the other with less powerful organizations with which one has elected to affiliate oneself. Ironically government and business take on some of the attributes of the divine - power, inevitability, and an inexorable and seemingly natural logic. Family and religion, for adults, provide opportunities for curbing the macro organizations' claims upon one's energies, time, and attention. Family and religion sector off a private sphere of life into which any involvement by a macro organization would be understood to be an encroachment or an invasion of privacy. It is in this private sphere that the individual can maintain a modicum of personal independence and even resistance against the imperialization of the macro organizations. Far from making the spiritual side of life irrelevant (as we would believe from many sermons), for most people the sectoring off of the public from the religious sphere, the compartmentalization of Sunday (or Saturday) from the rest of the week, is experienced as protecting an endangered chance at spiritual survival. It is a "privatized"[10] and therefore limited spirituality that survives, but it is feared that the alternative would be no spirituality at all.

So long as the "weighty" matters of social life are associated with the macro institutions and organizations from which religion and the other micro institutions and organizations are sectored off, the individual's sense of significance is going to be tied up experientially with the secular side of life. Religion consequently is distant from much that people are required to do in everyday life and from most of the important aspects of life. Rather religion inheres in the residual traces of one's own early childhood imagery and in the imagery that one might oneself cultivate in the lives of the next generation of children. Neither of these associations is particularly relevant to the later part of adulthood. Consequently for many people a renewed involvement in religion in old age requires a discovery of a non-childhood centered religiosity. Absent such a discovery, a religious involvement could be mere "playing at" religion. The fact that many people find religion important in old age suggests that a certain amount of discovery or learning takes place. Somehow one's individual sense of significance comes to be tied up experientially with a micro institution rather than a macro one.

Individual versus Community

People today generally experience social life as individuals rather than as members of a community. A community, in the strict sense of that term, is a social grouping that encompasses all or most of the facets of its members' lives. In a village community, for example, the residents of the village work, recreate, and worship together; they may not even know anybody well who does not live in the village. Even the contemporary small town is not a true community in the way the village was in former times. The village may have had seasonal celebrations in which the whole village participated in a ceremony. Much that we are accustomed to observing through the print and electronic media - national political and athletic spectacles, for example - had local counterparts that engaged village community members actively on a first-hand basis rather than through the media. In contemporary society, in contrast, people do not live in true communities; they typically work with one set of people, spend what little leisure time they have with another set of people, and worship, if they do so, with yet a third set of people. Leisure and worship gatherings may include the family members, but that is not necessarily the case since different family members may elect to participate in different churches or not to participate in a religious organization at all. For men in particular, as we suggested in Chapter 2, there may be some overlap between the work and leisure networks of people; however, there is not a community in the sense of a limited number of people who are involved in all aspects of one another's lives. Moreover the family is sectored off in most cases from the individual's work world.

There is a kind of social situation in the contemporary world that is similar to the true community insofar as it is not limited to one facet of the individual's life. In being non-purposive, a social network can be sufficiently different from the work place association of people that it might be experienced as something like a community. It is this kind of experience that church leaders try to encourage in their congregations when they endeavor to "build a community" or cultivate a "family spirit." The experience for the individual is not really family-like, insofar as the interpersonal activity is episodic and not tied to a common residence; but it is far from being the purpose-specific isolated involvement that is characteristic of a work place. It differs from the experience of the work place because it potentially involves any number of the dimensions of the individual as a person while the work place typically highlights only one or a few dimensions as relevant.

Because the societally important facets of one's life, which are frequently tied up with macro organizations, involve us as individuals rather than as communities, and only one or a few dimensions of the individual at that, the seemingly important features of our identities are based on our individualizing rather than communalizing activities. We allow work related roles in particular to become master statuses, controlling many of the other aspects of our lives. People want to know "what we do" for a living. We sacrifice the other aspects of our lives in order to live up to the demands of the master status. Our sense of self that may be built up in the few rather narrow roles becomes a pervasive background that provides a context for what we may be or do at home, church, or elsewhere. It is the very imperialistic nature of such individualizing roles, their potential for invading other aspects of life under the guise of our identities, that makes a retirement from them in later adulthood so problematic.

When older people find social support in a church "community" (more precisely, a church-based network), they are experiencing something different from what they had become accustomed to in the earlier phases of their adult lives. The building up of an identity on the basis of accomplishments will no longer be there. The addiction to power (or resisting power) will not be satisfied. Even the joys of "getting away" will no longer retain their previous quality, if for no reason other than there is no longer anything to get away from. Much that was once background to everything else will not be there except as an increasingly distant memory. What to expect from the congregational "community" and how to contribute to it needs to be learned, and for many people it needs to be learned for the first time. The transition cannot be expected to be an easy one. This is what ministers to older persons need to deal with when they "build up a community."

Being Ministered To Versus Ministering

Given the development of adult personalities in secular spheres rather than in religious contexts, and given their development on the basis of individualizing accomplishments rather than communal identity groups, the prospect of churches providing a social context for the subjective well-being of older persons suggests considerable adaptation on the part of the latter. Such adaptation is by no means impossible, but it should be recognized from the outset that it is not for everybody. Some people cannot be expected to rekindle a religious interest of any significance or authenticity. Others may not find any point to the formation of a non-purposeful "community" life. For those who do adjust to the congregational setting as a situation in life, the very adjustment process itself may contribute to mental well-being by reawakening the person as a balanced entity in which no one aspect of life crowds other aspects out.

The idea that people are going to begin "being ministered to" at an arbitrary point in life is entirely unrealistic. Rather those many people who have been "engulfed" in work and family roles for four decades or so will continue to seek ways to individualize themselves in purposeful roles; they will use the quasi-community experience that a church can provide to identify services that they might perform and to find opportunities to develop a more adult religiosity than may have emerged in their childhood years. Undertaking ministries is a way that older members of congregations can render service in a quasi-community context and find reason to develop a more sophisticated service-oriented spirituality. For many people, being ministered to by the congregation during the last stages of life cannot itself have much importance because the congregation was never important to them in the past. Their undertaking a ministry in the congregation will make the congregation itself important to them. In time they can build up a sense of the self being a part of the congregation, as they undertake that ministry. If religion and congregational life had been "unimportant" throughout a person's adult life, religious gestures from a church at the point in time when one is about to die could hardly be very consoling. If, however, one has come to experience the congregation of a church as important in the course of contributing to the congregation's life, the presence of congregation members during the last stage of life will be very meaningful. In the next chapter we will explore the congregational context for older people, as we found it to exist in a 1997 study of the Nashville, Tennessee, area's congregations.

Notes

1. For a general social scientific account of ambivalence, as the term is being used here, see Andrew J. Weigert, *Mixed Emotions. Certain Steps Toward Understanding Ambivalence* (Albany: State University of New York Press, 1991).

2. Weigert, *Mixed Emotions*, p. 88.

3. It is true, however, that one of the symptoms of clinical depression, an internal condition, is an inability to make decisions and that such an inability can engender ambivalent feelings.

4. The situation is analogous to what pollsters call "cross pressures."

5. Sociologists tend to conceptualize in terms of pure cases or "ideal types" and then use the types as yard sticks, as it were, that apply to real cases to greater and lesser extents.

6. Here we are adopting the phenomenologists' practice of using the first person singular in statements to present typical experiences.

7. As university professors, one of the strange situations we observe in the younger generation is a tendency to credit or blame government for what in fact big business does - set insurance premiums, charge prices for objects in retail establishments, and require various kinds of educational credential for work. Obviously, the relationships among the major institutions of our society are not transparent to many people.

8. Anthony J. Blasi, "Power, Class, Law: The Complementarity of Realpolitik and Soft Sociologies." *Sociologia Internationalis* 32:1 (1994): 47-54.

9. C. Wright Mills, *The Power Elite* (New York: Oxford University Press, 1956), saw the dominant institutions of his day as big business, big government, and big military.

10. The thesis that contemporary religion is privatized has been set out by Thomas Luckmann, *The Invisible Religion. The Problem of Religion in Modern Society.* New York: Macmillan, 1967.

Ch. 6 What Churches Do

We have seen the typical problems that older people encounter and the effect these problems can have in the form of clinical depression and the symptoms that often accompany that condition. We have also seen that religiosity, especially private religiosity, lessens depression and its symptoms, largely but not completely by occasioning perceptible social support. The perception of social support can improve morale by itself, making it less possible that the individual will become depressed. Together with subjective religiosity it may moderate the impact of problems by placing them in an interpreted framework in which they loom as less significant than such larger issues as salvation and the meaning of life. In the present chapter we will explore what the churches that often embody religion for people bring to the older people whom they serve. We will look at their resources, services, and opportunities for the older members of the congregations to provide services to one another.

A. Nashville and the U.S.

Our information comes from an interview survey of clergy and lay ministers to older persons in a sample of 25% of the congregations in the Nashville, Tennessee, metropolitan area.[1] A first preliminary question is, How applicable are findings from such a sample to the whole nation? To ascertain how much a Nashville study can tell us about the Mid-South of the United States or even about the country at large, we need to place Nashville in the national context and to make some comparisons between Nashville and the nation. The 1990 U.S. Census placed the population count of the Nashville

Metropolitan Statistical Area (Davidson County and the counties economically tied to it) at just under a million people (985,026).[2] As a central city, Nashville itself is the 24th largest city in population size in the United States; it grew by 8.6% between 1980 and 1992. Nashville is not very densely settled as cities go, with 1,046 people per square mile (73rd in density out of 77 cities of 200,000 or more people in the country). The city itself ranked 43rd out of 77 in the percentage of people aged 65 and over (11.4%) and 55th out of the 77 in the rate of crime.[3] Thus the city seems to be a typical one in terms of its percentage of older people and somewhat safer than most cities in terms of its crime rate.

In 1990 83.1% of the people in the Nashville Standard Metropolitan Area were white, compared to 80.3% of the nation's population, and 15.5% of the people in the SMA were African American, compared to 12.1% in the nation. Only 0.7% of Nashville's population was of "Hispanic origin" of whatever race, compared to 9.0% for the nation. Nashville also had fewer in the "Asian or Pacific Islander" category (1.0%) and "American Indian, Eskimo, or Aleut" category (0.2%), compared to the nation at large (2.9% and 0.8% respectively). Our informal impression is that Nashville will more closely match the rest of the nation in its racial and ethic composition in the 2000 Census. The 1990 Census reported a median annual household income level for Nashville ($30,223) that was very close to that of the nation ($30,056) and a median annual family income ($35,797) that was also close to the national median ($35,225). Slightly fewer of Nashville's families (8.6%) and individuals (11.3%) were reported below the poverty level in the 1990 Census than was the case for the nation (10.0% and 13.1% respectively).[4] In general population characteristics, Nashville seems to be typical of the nation, save being less affected in 1990 by recent trends in international migration. In terms of denominational affiliation, it resembles the rest of the East South Central region of the nation in being less Catholic and more Southern Baptist and Black Baptist than the rest of the nation (see Table 6.1).[7] It is different from both the region and the nation in having a higher proportion of Churches of Christ congregations.

Table 6.1: Per Cent of Total Adherents[5]

	U.S.	East South Central[6]	Davidson Co.
AME Zion	0.8	2.2	0.1
American Baptist	1.4	0.1	0.6
Assembly of God	1.6	1.3	1.2
Baptist - Black	6.4	10.8	14.9
Baptist - Southern	13.8	45.4	31.5
Catholic	38.9	7.4	7.3
Christian (Disciples)	0.8	1.0	1.0
Christian Brethen	0.1	--.-	0.1
Christian Churches	0.9	1.3	0.2
Church of God - Anderson	0.2	0.3	0.1
Church of God - Cleveland	0.5	1.4	0.4
Church of God of Prophecy	0.1	0.2	0.1
Church of Jesus Christ LDS	2.6	0.6	0.5
Church of the Nazarene	0.6	0.7	2.2
Churches of Christ	1.2	4.4	12.9
Cumberland Presbyterian	0.1	0.6	1.4
Episcopal	1.8	1.2	2.2
Ev. Luth. Ch. in America	3.8	0.3	0.6
Free Will Baptist	0.2	0.8	0.8
Independent Charismatic	0.6	0.4	1.3
Independent - other	0.9	1.1	0.7
Lutheran - Missouri	1.9	0.4	0.4
Lutheran - Wisconsin	0.3	--.-	0.1
Missionary Baptist "old"	--.-	0.2	0.8
Presbyterian - American	0.2	0.5	0.6
Presbyterian U.S.A.	2.6	1.8	3.5
Salvation Army	0.1	0.1	0.1
Seventh-day Adventists	0.7	0.6	1.6
Unitarian	0.1	--.-	0.1
United Church of Christ	1.5	0.2	0.1
United Methodist	8.1	12.1	11.5
Wesleyan	0.2	0.1	0.1

B. Representativeness of the Interview Sample

A second preliminary question is, How well does our 25% sample of congregations reflect the whole population of Nashville area churches? One way of addressing this question of representativeness is to compare information we have on the congregations that were not included in the sample with the ones that were included. The more similar the two bodies of information on the churches are, the better the representativeness of the survey. This kind of comparison requires information that is available for both the congregations that are not in the sample and those that are. Fortunately, we have information that enables us to make such comparisons.

One item of information that we have about every known church in the Nashville area is its location. With this simple piece of information we were able to find the 1990 census tract in which each church was situated; this in turn enabled us to look up the income per person for each church's tract.[8] We were also able to find the names of the senior pastors of most of the congregations and then find the home addresses of many of these people in telephone directories, city directories, and internet reference services. This enabled us to locate their home addresses in census tracts and find the 1990 incomes per person for those tracts. Table 6.2 presents the "average" or mean 1990 tract incomes per capita for the churches and for the known pastors' places of residence for the largely African American and largely white congregations included and not included in the interview sample. The mean incomes per capita do not differ substantially between the sampled and non-sampled congregations. This argues favorably for the representativeness of our sample.

Another item of information that we have for all of these congregations is some indication of any denominational affiliation that they may have. Nashville has a very complex denominational structure, with no less than fifty-one denominational categories.[9] Only three denominations have more than ten percent of the metropolitan area's congregations - the Churches of Christ with 12.8%, the Southern Baptist Convention with 12.5%, and the Missionary Baptists with 11.7%.[10] Since congregations tend to be larger in some denominations

Table 6.2: Census Tract Income Per Capita Means

Congregations	Church Tracts (N)	Pastors' Residence Tracts (N)
Largely African American		
Sample	$ 8,215 (51)	$11,725 (42)
Non-sample	$ 8,508 (162)	$11,533 (99)
Largely white		
Sample	$17,001 (131)	$16,640 (92)
Non-sample	$15,041 (374)	$17,719 (100)

than others, these figures should not be understood to reflect the metropolitan area's denominational membership totals but only congregations of differing sizes. Table 6.3 reports the percentage of congregations affiliated with each of the denominations in the total population of churches, in the African American sample, in the white sample, and in the two samples combined. The right hand column presents the percentage differences between the total population and the combined samples; the small sizes of these differences is a non-technical indicator that the sample closely reflects the denominational breakdown of the total population of congregations.

The Churches of Nashville

The number of different Christian denominations that are present in the Nashville metropolitan area make it difficult to describe the local church presence in a sentence or two. To simplify the picture, it is useful to categorize the denominations in a few types and to distinguish between the largely African American and the largely white (or majority) congregations. The categories that we found to be useful are charismatic, conservative, and other. The charismatic denominations are those whose congregational worship is marked by "speaking in tongues' (glossolalia) and a generally experientially-centered tone. The moral code is sometimes less ascetic than that of the conservatives. The conservative denominations are those who resolve all issues by referring to the Bible, whose congregational worship culminates in the preaching of the Word, and whose moral

Organized Religions and Seniors' Mental Health

6.3: Denominational Breakdowns - Population and Samples

Denomination	A % Total Popula-tion(N)	B % African American Sample(N)	C % White Sample(N)	D % Combined Samples(N)	A - D
Apostolic	1.0 (7)	2.0 (1)	0.8 (1)	1.1 (2)	- 0.1
Assembly	1.5 (11)	---	1.5 (2)	1.1 (2)	0.4
Baptist (Afr. Amer.)	2.2 (16)	5.9 (3)	---	1.6 (3)	0.6
Baptist (white)	3.9 (28)	---	3.8 (5)	2.7 (5)	1.2
Baptist- Free Will	2.5 (18)	---	3.8 (5)	2.7 (5)	- 0.2
Baptist - General	0.4 (3)	---	0.8 (1)	0.5 (1)	- 0.1
Baptist - Missionary	11.7 (84)	35.3(18)	---	9.9 (18)	1.8
Baptist - Primitive	2.5 (18)	9.8 (5)	---	2.7 (5)	- 0.2
Baptist - Southern	12.5 (90)	---	19.1(25)	13.7 (25)	- 1.2
Bible	0.3 (2)	---	0.8 (1)	0.5 (1)	- 0.2
Catholic	1.9 (14)	2.0 (1)	3.1 (4)	2.7 (5)	- 0.8
Charismatic	0.1 (1)	---	0.8 (1)	0.5 (1)	- 0.4
Christian	0.6 (4)	---	1.5 (2)	1.1 (2)	- 0.5

Organized Religions and Seniors' Mental Health

Table 6.3: Denominational Breakdowns - Population and Samples Cont'd.

Denomination	A % Total Popula-tion(N)	B % African American Sample(N)	C % White Sample(N)	D % Com-bined Samples(N)	A - D
Christian - Disciples	1.3 (9)	---	1.5 (2)	1.1 (2)	0.2
Christian Reformed	0.1 (1)	---	---	---	0.1
Christian Science	0.1 (1)	---	0.8 (1)	0.5 (1)	- 0.4
Church of God	2.1(15)	---	1.5 (2)	1.1 (2)	1.0
Church of God - And	0.3 (2)	---	0.8 (1)	0.5 (1)	- 0.2
Church of God in Christ	1.3 (9)	---	---	---	1.3
Church of God of Pro	0.1(1)	---	0.8 (1)	0.5 (1)	- 0.4
Church of J.C.- LDS	0.4(3)	---	---	---	0.4
Churches of Christ	12.8 (92)	5.9 (3)	15.3 (20)	12.6 (23)	0.2
Community	0.3 (2)	---	0.8 (1)	0.5 (1)	- 0.2
Episcopal	1.9 (14)	2.0 (1)	2.3 (3)	2.2 (4)	- 0.3
Episcopal - Southern	0.1 (1)	---	0.8 (1)	0.5 (1)	- 0.4
Evangelical Free Ch	0.1 (1)	---	---	---	0.1
Four Square Gospel	0.3 (2)	---	0.8 (1)	0.5 (1)	- 0.2
Friends	0.1 (1)	---	---	---	0.1

Organized Religions and Seniors' Mental Health

Table 6.3: Denominational Breakdowns - Population and Samples Cont'd.

Denomination	A % Total Popula-tion(N)	B % African American Sample(N)	C % White Sample(N)	D % Com-bined Samples(N)	A - D
Independent	5.1 (37)	11.8 (6)	3.1 (4)	5.5 (10)	- 0.4
Interdenominational	1.8 (13)	---	3.1 (4)	2.2 (4)	- 0.4
Jehovah's Witness	1.1 (8)	---	1.5 (2)	1.1 (2)	0.0
Lutheran - ECLA	0.8 (6)	---	0.8 (1)	0.5 (1)	0.3
Lutheran - MO & WI	1.0 (7)	---	1.5 (2)	1.1 (2)	-0.1
Mennonite	0.1 (1)	---	---	---	0.1
Methodist - AME	1.7 (12)	7.8 (4)	---	2.2 (4)	- 0.5
Methodist - CME	0.7 (5)	3.9 (2)	---	1.1 (2)	- 0.4
Methodist - Southern	0.4 (3)	---	0.8 (1)	0.5 (1)	-0.1
Methodist - United	8.8 (63)	5.9 (3)	9.9 (13)	8.8 (16)	0.0
Nazarene	3.6 (26)	---	5.3 (7)	3.8 (7)	- 0.2
Orthodox	0.3 (2)	---	0.8 (1)	0.5 (1)	- 0.2
Pentecostal	4.2 (30)	3.9 (2)	3.1 (4)	3.3 (6)	0.9
Presbyterian	0.7 (5)	---	0.8 (1)	0.5 (1)	0.2
Presbyterian -Amer	0.7 (5)	---	0.8 (1)	0.5 (1)	0.2
Presbyterian -Cumb	1.8 (13)	---	2.3 (3)	1.6 (3)	0.2

Organized Religions and Seniors' Mental Health

Table 6.3: Denominational Breakdowns - Population and Samples Cont'd.

Denomination	A % Total Popula-tion(N)	B % African American Sample(N)	C % White Sample(N)	D % Com-bined Samples(N)	A - D
Presbyterian -U	2.9 (21)	0.0 (1)	3.1 (4)	2.7 (5)	0.2
Seventh-day Adventist	0.6 (4)	0.0 (1)	0.8 (1)	1.1 (2)	- 0.5
Unitarian	0.3 (2)	---	---	---	0.3
United Church of Christ	0.4 (3)	---	0.8 (1)	0.5 (1)	- 0.1
Unity	0.1 (1)	---	---	---	0.1
Unity - Independent	0.1 (1)	---	---	---	0.1
Wesleyan	0.3 (2)	---	0.8 (1)	0.5 (1)	- 0.2

code is sometimes more ascetic than that found in the Bible. The "other" category of denominations includes the liturgical churches, the ones that emphasize ritual in their worship services (e.g., Evangelical Lutheran Church in America, Episcopal, Catholic, and Orthodox), and the theologically liberal churches (e.g., Presbyterian U.S.A., United Church of Christ, and United Methodist). Even using these broad categories, there are some churches that do not neatly fit into any type. Table 6.4 presents the distribution of Nashville's Christian congregations among these broad types of denomination, distinguishing the largely African American and the largely white congregations. One striking feature of the distribution is the similarity of the African American and white percentages. A second feature is the dominance of the conservative denominations in the metropolitan area, along with a strong presence of the "other" category. Both of these features should dispel the stereotype of worship in the African American churches and churches in the South generally, being exclusively experience-centered.

Table 6.4: Distribution of Congregations among Tradition Types in
the Nashville Sample
Tradition % (N)

Population	Charismatic	Conservative	Other	N.A.
African American	3.9 (2)	58.8 (30)	23.5(12)	13.7 (7)
White	9.8 (13)	57.1 (76)	26.3(35)	6.8 (9)

Another way to look at the variations among the congregations is to look at the way their denominations are organized. If a congregation is not really connected to other congregations by some structure, more local initiative may be required from the members, old and young alike, simply to provide a minimum program of worship. Sometimes there is a weak connectedness through a denominational structure, but that connectedness may depend either more upon the association of non-ordained members or upon the associations of ordained clergy. The everyday experience of a church can be quite different in these two settings, even though both are "weakly connected." Some denominations are strongly connected; the local congregation occasions an encounter with a "brand name," so to speak (e.g., "Lutheran" or "Catholic"). A minister can call upon the help of a denominational agency in these cases. In Table 6.5 we see that the charismatic congregations are entirely in denominations having weak denominational structures that maintain affiliations largely through the ordained clergy and that the "other" (liturgical and liberal denomination) congregations are almost entirely in strongly connected denominational structures. The conservative congregations tend to be found in the weakly connected structures that are maintained through the clergy, much like the charismatics; however, some are weakly connected largely through lay associations. The congregations that do not fit neatly into any one type are largely independents; per definition they are unconnected.

Table 6.5: Distribution of Congregations among Types of
Denominational Polity,
By Tradition Types

Polity %   (N)

Population	Unconnected	Weakly-lay	Weakly-clergy	Strongly
Charismatic	----	----	100.0 (14)	----
Conservative	1.9 (2)	22.6(24)	59.4 (63)	16.0(17)
Other	----	----	4.3 (2)	95.7(45)
N.A.	94.1(16)	5.9 (1)	----	----

We will be using the tradition type categories through part of our inquiry because they indicate the kind of experience that many readers can identify. They also indicate the resources that the congregations bring to their older members. The charismatic churches may occasion an experience that is or could be termed "emotionally satisfying." The liturgical and liberal churches may bring highly trained clergy (and other ministers) as well as denominational agencies to the service of older persons. The weakly connected lay-centered congregations - some 22.6% of the conservative congregations - offer opportunities for older persons (usually older men) to perform active organizational roles.[11] The weakly connected pastor-centered type, including a majority of the conservative congregations and all of the charismatic ones, may occasion the entry of the pastor into the lives of the older members as a significant personage.

Older People in the Nashville Churches

The congregations in Nashville (and elsewhere) vary by size. What the real size of any given congregation might be is difficult to ascertain, and making valid comparisons from one congregation to another is even more difficult. What constitutes membership differs from one denomination to another; in some cases children, who may have been baptized as infants, are counted as members while sometimes they are not. Many congregations do not have a sufficient staff to maintain updated records of which members may have moved out of town or perhaps died without anyone notifying their former church's office. Sometimes people change churches without notifying the one with which they are no longer effectively affiliated. Moreover, many people begin attending a local church without formalizing an affiliation in any way.[12] For purposes of making reasonably valid comparisons, finding out how many people actually attend Sunday (or Saturday, in the case of the Seventh-day Adventists) services is a more statistically sound procedure.

Some older people who play important roles in the life of a local congregation may not be present at the weekly worship services. They may be home-bound or in a nursing home and may be incapacitated and thus unable to attend a church. Nevertheless, they may receive regular visits from the congregation's minister to the elderly, may maintain a correspondence or phone ministry of their own focused on encouraging other congregation members, may be part of a network of people who pray for one another, or may be mentioned on a regular basis at the worship services. A team of younger members in the congregation may even help maintain such a person's residence or help the person financially. For this reason it seemed best to ask the ministers whom we interviewed (clergy and lay ministers to older people) how many *members* of their congregations were aged 65 and over, even though we gauged the size of the congregations themselves with *attendance* figures.

Table 6.6: Older Persons in Sampled Nashville Congregations

Tradition or Population	Mean Number of Older Persons*			Mean Attendance	Elderly/Attend Ratio
	Black	White	Total		
Charismatic	21.5 (2)	14.9 (13)	15.8 (15)	95.0	0.166
Conservative	43.0 (30)	88.9 (76)	75.9 (106)	251.1	0.302
Other	41.8 (12)	131.9 (35)	108.9 (47)	289.8	0.376
N.A.	10.0 (7)	34.8 (9)	22.5 (17)	490.5	0.046
Total	37.3 (51)	89.3 (133)	74.5 (185)	270.3	0.276
African American			37.3 (51)	161.4	0.231
White			89.3 (133)	313.6	0.285

*Number of congregations in parentheses

Table 6.6 shows that the average service attendance in a Nashville congregation is approximately 270 people and that the average number of members aged 65 or above is about 75 people. Creating a ratio out of these two figures (74.5 /270.3) yields a figure of 0.276. However the charismatic churches are much smaller than the others and can be expected to have greater difficulty supplying services that depend on scale - e.g., having a full time minister to older people (versus a full-time pastor or a part time person ministering to older people). Similarly the largely African American congregations are smaller than the white congregations. The ratio of elderly membership to attendance does not differ much between the largely African American and white congregations, but it is a much lower figure for the charismatic churches; this suggests that the typical person aged 65 years or higher in a charismatic church could be integrated into the lives of younger people (e.g., their children's generation) by the church but not readily made part of a social network of other older people. The conservative and the "other" (liturgical and liberal) churches can more readily maintain social groups, study groups, and ministry teams of older persons.

An interesting question is, What kind of problems do persons aged 65 and above in the differing congregations in Nashville have? Do they bring the problems they have to the congregations' ministers to older people or do they hide some problems and bring a few selected kinds of problem? Because we are not reporting the results of a needs survey based on interviews with the older persons themselves, we cannot address this matter directly. However, when we interviewed the ministers to older people to whom older persons had spoken about some anxiety-producing problem in the previous month and asked them what kind of problem the person(s) had, family problems seemed to be troubling people in the congregations located in lower income areas and medical problems seemed more prevalent in the higher income areas. To examine this more closely, we calculated the average census tract incomes per capita for the congregations whose ministers to the elderly reported the different kinds of problem (see Table 6.7). Among the largely African American congregations there was no clear pattern, but there was also less of a spread among those churches in their census tracts' income per capita. Among the largely white congregations and in the total sample, the combination of financial and medical problems appears in higher income areas while the combination of financial and family problems appears in the lower income areas. Medical problems that lead to the necessity of moving to a nursing home could be expected to necessitate financial adjustments (if not occasion problems) among even very prosperous populations, while at the other end of the financial spectrum the severe financial problems of people residing in low income areas can be expected to take their toll on family relationships. In one setting, the older person may turn to the church when a medical problem occasions a loss of financial independence; in the other setting, the older person turns to the church when poverty strains the family.

Table 6.7: Census Tract Income Per Capita Means
By Kinds of Older Persons' Problem Brought to Ministers

Kinds of Problem	African American Congregations Congregations	White Congregations	Total
Financial & Medical	---- (1)	$23,614 (5)	$22,587 (6)
Medical & Family	$ 7,716 (8)	$17,785 (32)	$15,771 (40)
Medical	$ 8,761 (13)	$17,209 (29)	$14,594 (42)
Financial	---- (1)	$16,021 (3)	$14,148 (4)
Family	$ 8,799 (6)	$15,472 (19)	$13,871 (25)
Financial, Medical, & Family	$ 7,182 (5)	$14,627 (11)	$12,300 (16)
Financial & Family	$ 4,991 (4)	$14,404 (5)	$10,220 (9)
NA	$ 7,726 (12)	$16,320 (29)	$14,454 (42)

Church Programs for and by Older Persons

The most common response of the Nashville churches for the specific needs of older persons is to organize visits. It may be the pastor who visits the home-bound or those in nursing homes, but especially in the larger congregations there may be another minister who does this. In a few cases the church arranges for children to visit nursing homes. Because the number of older persons under care in their own homes has grown, they are no longer centralized as often in nursing homes. Thus another pattern commonly found in the congregations seems to be particularly appropriate: a team of older people who are in good health visit those who are not in good health. The more liturgically oriented churches will use the bringing of communion as an occasion for a visit. While confinement at home or in a medical facility brings with it the danger of isolation from friends and family, it also keeps the individual away from the church program of activities. In response some pastors conduct separate services in nursing homes and assisted living facilities and some congregations arrange for church music to be played or sung in those settings.

The second most common response to the needs of older persons, found in almost all of the larger congregations, consists of a seniors' fellowship group that organizes entertainments, trips, dinners, craft clubs, and informational seminars on such diverse topics as wills, finances, taxes, medical problems, crime, nutrition, and safety. In addition, the seniors' groups may undertake a number of specialized ministries - visiting or preparing meals for those who are incapacitated, housing street people, working as volunteers in shelters, collecting used clothing and furniture for the needy, and so forth. In many cases these ministries by older people may continue for an indefinite period because of the individual initiative of a member of the congregation who began doing such things in a fellowship group context. Consider the following field note that appears on the back side of one of our interview pages:

> R (a lay volunteer in his seventies) is short of breath and slow moving, as if suffering from a congestive heart problem; however, he was clearly on top of matters mentally and could use his

> experience in his unofficial work to good
> advantage.

What R (the respondent being interviewed) did in his church was visit every older person he heard might need help, assess the situation, and arrange for whatever might be needed - money, legal help, food, work on a home, transportation, etc. In another church, whose congregation consisted almost entirely of older people, we interviewed two septuagenarians in a church kitchen area:

> The ministries to the elderly and to the poor appear
> to be undertaken by the congregation, which has a
> tradition of charitable works.

The congregation was operating a soup kitchen, shelter for the homeless, clothing center, and other good works for the poor. It is often difficult to distinguish ministry to and ministry by the older congregation members; their works no doubt contribute to their own mental well-being.

A number of church responses to the needs of older members centered around food. Several pastors reported having a regularly scheduled dinner with an informal group of elderly people. A number of congregations had special dinners either in honor of the older members of the congregation or put on by them. Sometimes help for the partially incapacitated elderly involved providing meals on a regular basis, usually as part of a meals on wheels program though sometimes informally. Some churches maintain a food bank or purchase food for somebody.

Other frequent kinds of response to the needs of older people involve regular phone calls to check up on the well-being and needs of older congregation members, correspondence ministries by older members to help maintain contact with the less healthy, Sunday school classes made up almost entirely by the older members, middle of the week Bible study groups that turn out *de facto* to be for the older members, committees that plan programs specifically for the elderly, volunteer groups often including youths who help maintain older members' residences, financial help in emergencies, and transportation to church and to physician appointments. Because one of the problems older people face is the loss of a spouse, some churches organize grief support groups and provide help with funerals. A few churches organize fitness groups for seniors. One pastor collects and stores medical equipment for loan largely to older people.

For some people, these church responses address practical needs for money, food, information, advice, transportation, and help. For many, it would appear to be a matter of removing small worries and preventing neglect. For others, these responses represent opportunities for the older members to become involved with others on an everyday basis by involving themselves in the ministries.

Ministers to Older Persons

In the smaller churches, a pastor often serves as the minister to older persons. This seems to be the case particularly in the largely African American congregations. The larger churches may have an associate pastor responsible for this ministry. In some instances a lay volunteer, either formally or informally, performs the role. In our interview sample of 185, the ministers to older persons in the Nashville churches have an average age of 52 years and on average have eighteen years (college degree plus two years) of formal education. About 87% are currently married. The congregations that are larger (as indicated by attendance figures) appear to be the ones that have full time ministers to older persons (see Table 6.8). In slightly more than half of the largely African American congregations the minister to older persons is not full time, while the figure is about 37% for the largely white congregations. The largely African American churches that have a full time person serving as the minister to older persons have more people aged 65 and above, on the average, than those that do not, while it is the largely white congregations that do not have a full time person serving in that capacity that have more persons aged 65 and above. These latter congregations also have ministers to older persons who are on the average older than their counterparts in other congregations.

One of the important functions that ministers to older persons perform in the congregations is "being there." Being there involves maintaining sufficient contact with the older members of the congregation and gaining their confidence so that they in fact

Organized Religions and Seniors' Mental Health

Table 6.8: Full- and Part-Time Ministers to Older Persons

Minister to Older Persons is Full Time (N)	Attendance (Mean)	Persons Aged 65+ (Mean N)	Ministers' Education (Mean Yrs.)	Ministers' Age (Mean Yrs.)	Available Substitute (Per cent)
Largely African American Churches					
Full-time (24)	211.4	46.7	17.7	49.5	95.8
Part-time (27)	117.0	29.0	17.6	50.9	81.5
Largely White Churches					
Full-time (86)	364.6	80.9	18.4	49.1	89.5
Part-time (47)	220.4	104.7	17.2	58.3	78.7
Total Sample of Churches					
Full-time (110)	331.1	73.5	18.2	49.2	90.9
Part-time (75)	181.0	76.1	17.3	55.2	78.7

speak freely about their problems and worries either with the minister or in the minister's presence. Being there also involves "building a community" or social network so that the ministers find out about problems even if the person needing attention does not personally bring it to a minister's attention. It is important that the older person's family also knows or at least knows of the ministers so that they can seek help for their older family members when help of that kind is needed. In order to obtain an indication of how much older members of the sampled congregations bring their problems or worries to the attention of the ministers to older persons (or if they are unable, have the experience of someone else bringing it to the minister's attention), we asked the ministers how many people aged 65 or above were members of their congregations and how many of those members had come (or had their problem brought) to the minister with an anxiety-producing problem or worry in the previous month. Then we formed a ratio of these two figures, which we call a "seek rate." The seek rake is the fraction of older congregation members whose worry or problem the ministers were dealing with in some way in the past month, even if what the ministers were doing was merely a matter of listening and encouraging. We also asked the ministers whether the older members of the congregation came to them with their problems or worries "often," "sometimes," or "never." Table 6.9, which presents the seek rate averages for the three possible answers to that question, appears to validate the seek rate as a meaningful indicator.

Table 6.9: Seek Rate By How Often Older Persons Bring Problems

How Often	Seek Rate Mean	(Number of Interviews)
Often	0.15	(74)
Sometimes	0.12	(85)
Never	0.00	(9)

$p = .02$

As indicated by the "seek rate," in the African American context older members of congregations in the liturgical and liberal ("other") denominations appear to bring their problems and worries to the minister to older persons more often than is the case in the conservative denominations; by contrast in the white context the older members in the charismatic congregations appear to be more likely to do so than either the conservative or "other" denominations. However, the pattern is not very dramatic (see Table 6.10), and only the tendency apparent in the total sample for the charismatic denominations' seek rate to be higher is unlikely to be a product of random chance.

Table 6.10: Seek Rate By Population Context and Tradition Type

Tradition Type	Largely African American Congregations	Largely White Congregations	Total Sample*
Charismatic	---- (1)	0.166 (13)	0.158 (14)
Conservative	0.111 (28)	0.118 (71)	0.116 (99)
Other	0.145 (12)	0.095 (35)	0.108 (47)
N.A.	0.296 (4)	0.183 (7)	0.224 (11)

* p less than .01, exclusive of the N.A. row

One of the resources that ministers to older people bring to their congregations is a knowledge about and even familiarity with mental health specialists and other professionals. It is particularly important for ministers to find specialists who are helpful and whom they can both consult and to whom they may refer people. It is especially helpful if they can find specialists who are reasonably sympathetic to the religious tradition in question. In order to help describe the familiarity on the part of the ministers to older people with appropriate specialists, we asked them whose advice they might seek when dealing with an older person who seemed especially tense, distressed, depressed, or even suicidal. Table 6.11 shows that the ministers to older persons who seek advice from psychologists and psychiatrists or who named multiple kinds of specialist (depending on the nature of the problem) had, on the average, the highest levels of formal educational attainment. The ministers who seek advice from social workers, counselors, or physicians have slightly less educational attainment; it is notable that many of these ministers mention agencies that are staffed by social workers and counselors. The ministers who seek advice from people such as other clergy who are not mental health specialists or do not seek advice at all have on the average the least formal education. It seems that those who need access to advice the most have the fewest contacts for obtaining it.

Table 6.11: Educational Attainment and Percentage in Senior Pastors' Residential Census Tract with 16+ Years Education, By Advisor of Minister to Older Persons

Advisor	Mean Educational Attainment (N)	Mean% in Pastor's Tract with 16+ Years Education
Psychologist	20.1 (8)	29.8 (7)
Psychiatrist	20.0 (9)	25.7 (8)
Multiple	18.8 (27)	25.2 (19)
Social Worker	18.7 (9)	24.8 (7)
Counselor	18.2 (63)	26.5 (46)
Physician	17.9 (10)	18.4 (6)
None	16.7 (27)	16.1 (20)
Other	15.9 (32)	20.7 (25)

We wanted to know whether access to advice from specialists was a simple function of financial resources. When we looked at the per capita incomes of census tracts in which the churches were located, we found no particular pattern with the kinds of advisor mentioned by the ministers. Because some prosperous congregations have church buildings located in central lower income neighborhoods, we tried using the per capita incomes of the census tracts of the senior pastors' homes; there was still no clear pattern. However, when we looked at the average percentages of the adults in the senior pastors' residence census tracts who had sixteen or more years of formal education, a rough pattern emerged (see Table 6.11).[13] The senior pastors of those congregations whose ministers to older persons who had no specialist from whom they sought advice had on the average the lowest percentage of college educated neighbors (16.1%). Any lack of this kind of resource appears to be more directly related to class culture - as represented by environments that are characterized by less formal educational attainment - than a lack of financial resources. In terms of both the ministers' own educational attainment and the percentage of adults in the senior pastors' residential census tracts having sixteen or more years of education, the main difference seems to be that between those who seek advice from mental health specialists and social workers on the one hand and on the other those who seek advice from physicians, "others," or who seek no advice.

 We asked the ministers to the elderly to whom older persons had come (or been brought) with anxiety producing problems or worries during the previous month what they did in response. About 45% had occasion to refer an older person to some kind of specialist in the previous month. Making such a referral requires there to be a need for a referral in the eyes of the minister, a willingness and ability on the part of the minister to make the referral, and an absence of someone else (e.g., family members or the older persons themselves) already having made a referral. In Table 6.12 we see that the congregations in which the ministers made referrals in the previous month generally

Table 6.12: Congregations' Class Indicators By What Ministers to Older Persons Did When Problems Were Brought to Them

What Did	% (N)	Church Tract Income Per Capita	Church Tract Tract % with 16+ Yrs. Ed.	Sr. Pastor's Tract % with 16+ Yrs. Ed. (N)
Pray	1.4 (2)	$28,207	39.9	----
Encourage	3.5 (5)	$18,196	33.6	25.4 (4)
Combination - no refer	45.1(65)	$15,650	22.8	21.7 (48)
Combination - refer	38.2(55)	$13,146	21.6	27.2 (43)
Other	4.2 (6)	$12,746	17.8	36.1 (3)
Listen	7.6 (11)	$12,627	17.4	18.0 (8)
No problems brought	---- (41)	$14,258	20.4	21.0 (31)

were neither in the highest nor lowest income areas, as reflected in the churches' census tract per capita incomes and percentages of adults having sixteen or more years of education.   However, those congregations in which referrals were made averaged highest in their senior pastors' residence census tracts' percentages of adults having sixteen or more years of formal education. This too may be a class culture phenomenon - referrals in congregations whose seniors pastors live among more educated neighbors.   It is also interesting that ministers to older persons in the largely African American congregations made referrals in the previous month in 63.2% of the cases where the minister had dealt with a problem or worry of an older person, while the figure was only 29.3% in the largely white congregations; this is despite the the fact that the African American congregations tend to be smaller and hence would be expected statistically to have cases requiring referrals in fewer instances. It appears that the older members of high income census tract congregations may be referred to mental health and other specialists by family or may go to the specialists on their own. The more middle and working class congregations and the largely African American ones may depend on the ministers to the elderly to make referrals.   The ability of a congregation to retain a senior pastor who lives among highly educated neighbors seems to be related statistically to the actions of ministers to older persons making referrals; this may be a matter either of a large church supporting a senior pastor well and also having a minister to older persons on staff who is trained to make referrals, or a matter of a similarly trained part-time pastor who works in a secular occupation and does sufficiently well financially in that occupation to live among highly educated neighbors.

Conclusion

In 1990 Nashville was less affected by recent international migration than was the rest of the United States, but we suspect that it has become more like the rest of the nation in that respect in the subsequent years. Immigration historically brings in a relatively young population; consequently we can assume that the older population of Nashville is less ethnically varied than that of the United States as a whole. In its religious composition, Nashville is similar to the East

Central South part of the nation and unlike the rest of the nation in being less Catholic and more Southern Baptist and Black Baptist than the nation as a whole. It is unique in its higher population of Churches of Christ congregations. Findings derived from a Nashville study such as this one cannot be simply extrapolated to the rest of the nation, but they are by no means irrelevant to the larger picture. We have reason to believe that our 25% sample of congregations represents well those of the Nashville metropolitan area.

The particular kinds of religious tradition the various Christian churches in Nashville embody - charismatic, conservative, and "other" (liturgical and liberal) - is related to whether there are denomination-based counseling services for the church to bring to the needs of its older members. Without such denomination-based services, anything of that kind would have to be provided instead by the congregation itself. It is also related to whether any such services come through clergy connections or lay connections with a denominational central office. Generally, charismatic churches are weakly connected to one another through their clergy, the conservative churches weakly connected through the clergy or through lay associations, and the liturgical and liberal churches are strongly connected. The African American and white churches are similar in their distribution across the tradition types.

Older members of congregations have fewer associates in their age category in the charismatic churches and the greatest number in the predominantly white "other" (liturgical and liberal) churches. This is true both in terms of absolute numbers and in terms of ratios of older members to the Sunday (or in the case of the Seventh-day Adventists, Saturday) attendance figures. The church programs - both formally and *de facto* for or by the older members - vary considerably. Most common are visitation programs and fellowship groups, both often maintained by older members themselves. A particularly healthy phenomenon is older congregation members undertaking outreach volunteer programs to the poor and to the home bound.

The minister to older persons may be the church pastor, especially in the smaller churches; in some cases it may be a part-time pastor. In large churches an associate pastor or some other staff person, or a lay volunteer in the medium sized churches, may take on the responsibility of ministering to the older congregation members. A slightly higher proportion of older persons in the charismatic churches may come or be brought to the minister than in the conservative and "other" (liturgical and liberal) churches; this makes sense, given the lesser proportion of same-aged people and hence smaller natural support network older persons find in the charismatic churches.

In general the ministers to older persons bring two secular resources to their work - their own education and their familiarity with mental health specialists. Those having the least formal education of their own as a resource appear to have established the fewest working relationships with mental health specialists. The distance from the specialists is as much as if not more so a class cultural phenomenon as it is a matter of financial resources.

Notes

1. For details of the sampling methodology and the interview questions that were used, see Appendix Two at the end of this volume.

2. U.S. Bureau of the Census, *Census of Population and Housing. Nashville TN MSA* (Washington: U.S. Government Printing Office, 1993).

3. U.S. Bureau of the Census, *County and City Data Book 1994* (Washington: U.S. Government Printing Office, 1994).

4. *Census of Population and Housing. Nashville*; U.S. Bureau of the Census, *1990 Census of Population. Social and Economic Characteristics. United States* (Washington: U.S. Government Printing Office, 1993); and U.S. Bureau of the Census, *1990 Census of Population. General Population Characteristics. United States* (Washington: U.S. Government Printing Office, 1992).

5. Source: Martin B. Bradley et al., *Churches and Church Membership in the United States 1990* (Atlanta: Glenmary Research Center, 1992).

6. Includes Kentucky, Tennessee, Mississippi, and Alabama.

7. The denominational categories used in Table 6.1 differ from those used in our other tables.

8. A Nashville Metropolitan Planning Commission street index giving census tract numbers for street addresses was instrumental in this phase of the study, as was the Bureau of the Census volume with data on each census tract, *Census of Population and Housing. Nashville.* In a few cases it was necessary to refer to census tract boundary maps that had been drawn up for the 1990 census.

9. Note that the denominational categories used in our analysis differ from those given in Table 6.1, which are those used by the Glenmary Research

Center in Atlanta. Glenmary's data are limited more or less to denominations whose central offices cooperated in their project while we used whatever denominational identity local congregational officials, street signs, and directories provided. The main difficulty we encountered with our methodology is that a number of the largely African American Baptist churches were dually affiliated (i.e., they affiliated with more than one denominational association). We resolved the difficulty by including them in our "Baptist (African American)" category.

10. The Churches of Christ are a locally strong association of congregations in the Campbellite tradition; they have an affiliated university in Nashville. The Southern Baptist Convention is headquarted in the city and also has an affiliated university in the city. The Missionary Baptists locally are the largest identifiably African American denomination.

11. This is particularly the case of the lay officers termed "elders" (a direct translation of the New Testament term *presbyteroi*) in the Churches of Christ. In many cases the elders rotate responsibilities; one of these responsibilities is attending to the needs of older persons.

12. See Benson Y. Landis, "Confessions of a Church Statistician," in Louis Schneider (ed.), *Religion, Culture, and Society* (New York: Wiley, 1964), pp. 21-23.

13. In many cases, of course, the minister to older persons and the senior pastor were the same individual.

Ch. 7 Overview

We began this study with a consideration of the size and condition of the older population of the United States (and, by extension, modern industrialized societies like it). We observed that the older population, as defined by those people who are aged sixty-five and above, is increasing as a proportion of the total population. This growth was not simply an expansion in numbers of a kind of older population known before in history; a substantial qualitative change has also taken place. Because of the lengthening "health span" that has accompanied the lengthening of the life span, the older population is healthier than in the past and less often confined to institutionalized residential arrangements. Medical problems still beset older people, but it would be entirely misleading to associate the life circumstances of older people with a hospital-like environment. Similarly, because of Social Security and other employment-based retirement plans, the financial circumstances of many older people today are better than they were just a few decades ago. Problems nevertheless exist, especially for those who live alone. What has not really changed is the social meaning of the "old age" sector of the "life cycle." People lose the family role and occupational involvements that had engulfed them for most of their adult lives, and they rapidly become vulnerable to social isolation and loneliness.

Contemporary programs that are intended to respond to the needs of older persons seem to be modeled on the basis of images from the past. There is Medicare, the financial apparatus set up for purchasing medical treatments, and few people would want to do away with it. There are also pensions, including the Social Security system, based on past earnings. However, people do more than simply need food and shelter a short time after age sixty-five and then get sick and die. The necessity for the federal government to increase the funds available for the Social Security retirement system and the Medicare system and to introduce savings incentives into the federal tax code is only the first adjustment that needs be made in light of the changes associated with the longer life and health spans. The whole idea of "retirement," for example, needs to be reviewed. Should retirement be so abrupt? Or instead should pensions and Social Security be phased in more gradually and work more gradually phased down?

Such considerations raise dilemmas of all kinds. One of these dilemmas concerns part-time work. Some older people cannot make ends meet with retirement income, and a part-time job can be of great assistance financially. However, a job tacked onto the end of life without any connection with what came before would appear to be as much a disruption as a sudden retirement. There may not be any continuity in the new job with any training, career, or familiarity with work associates from the past. The job may actually take the individual away from any social network rather than help hold a network together. The importance of this increases because women as well as men entered the work force in large numbers, beginning in the 1970s, and are now expected to face the same "retirement" situation as men. We cannot propose to outline any comprehensive solution here, but we can point to the need to think within a framework that goes well beyond present programs and routines.

One element of life that can maintain some continuity across the different stages of a person's life is the religious dimension. One's religion can continue despite disruptions that may stem from retirement, loss of family role, or acquisition of some new fragmentary job experience. For this reason we described the inherent human capacity for religion, a capacity that can develop into different kinds of religious expression through the course of one's life. We noted, however, that the capacity for religion often remains underdeveloped, especially in the form of a childhood religiosity that remains more or less unchanged even while the individual undergoes other significant personal transformations. In other instances a personal religiosity may develop somewhat when the individual begins rearing children rather than being a child, but this too should be seen as appropriate for a stage of life, not life as a whole. A broader spirituality, one that can provide a perspective on the larger issues of life, seems to hold the greatest potential for helping the individual confront problems in old age.

Problems include conditions such as illness and low income but are not limited to those conditions. Problems, as we have used the term, also involve the individual interpreting the conditions as problems. Cultural resources such as religions that affect how someone interprets the environing world are important factors in the fashioning of either beneficial or harmful responses to difficulties. A religion that is so other-worldly as to lead the individual to neglect matters of health and finance can be detrimental rather than beneficial; a condition that begins as a problem that can be readily dealt with can worsen if neglected and become a serious problem that negatively affects the individual's subjective well-being. A religion that may not be other-worldly but is fatalistic, one that leaves the individual believing that nothing done in the face of problems matters, can similarly lead to inattention and neglect until matters become too serious to be dealt with adequately. A religion that encourages responsibility, however, can keep problems "in perspective" without leading to neglect. Such a religion may embody its stance in the saying, "God helps those who help themselves." The religious perspective goes beyond mere self-help by leading the individual's attention toward larger matters into which a problem may be placed and by leading the individual's attention towards other people. This directing of the individual's attention toward the divine (the "vertical dimension" of religion) and toward others (the "horizontal dimension" of religion), much in the manner of work, may prevent someone from morbidly dwelling on a problem to the point of turning inward or developing an entirely self-centered perspective.[1]

Seeing religion as a medicine would be inaccurate. If someone has not cultivated an active religiosity since childhood, one cannot expect it to have much effect on subjective well-being after problems have been allowed to become serious. Seeing religion as something that only other people do, even if one attends church regularly, similarly cannot be expected to have much impact on one's quality of life. It would be something like expecting to enjoy the benefits of exercise by effortlessly driving a motor vehicle to a stadium or turning on the television to watch professional athletes perform. Religion leads to beneficial effects by engaging the attention of the individual in activities. The activities may be cognitive or behavioral. Religious cognitive activity explores all aspects of life and develops as a habitual perspective that places everything within a larger context.

By its very nature, a perspective or environing context cannot take the form of an add-on or overlay, nor can a habitual perspective develop overnight. Because religions are shared traditions that build on the capacity developed in early childhood to see everything in terms of other persons, religious behavioral activity involves the individual with other people. Particularly important is the formation of small networks of people doing things within the congregational context. Such activity makes more sense in people's lives when they are in continuity with the person's long term commitments and follow naturally from the individual's identity as a religious person. Simply getting into an activity after problems have become serious will lack such important linkages, even if the individual is in any condition to begin being active.

When we measured older people's subjective well-being in terms of a scale of depression symptoms, we found that "private religion" and "perceived social support" both made a difference. Private religion - as indicated by the frequency with which older people read the Bible, talked about religion, prayed, and the like - was mildly related to, and perceived social support was strongly related to having fewer depression symptoms. Public religion was related to older white people perceiving themselves as enjoying greater social support while private religion was related to older African American people perceiving themselves as enjoying greater social support. Thus private religion seems to provide the benefit of buffering the effects of problems both directly and through its association with perceived social support; public religion seemed to provide that benefit largely for whites through an association with perceived social support. One cannot but help think of private religiosity in old age developing from a prior involvement in both public and private religiosity.

If contemporary social structures work against religion having an effective presence in people's lives, the contribution that religion can make to the subjective well-being of older persons is jeopardized. The question is not one of belief in the sense of assenting or not assenting to various doctrines that churches teach. For example, an agnostic or atheist can cultivate an other-centered perspective through humanistic endeavors. There are numerous non-theist philosophical perspectives that can contextualize problems and involve individuals in social networks that pursue worthwhile endeavors. Moreover, it is possible for some people to believe intellectually in God in a distant manner without developing the cognitive "habit" of placing all things within a theistic perspective or without engaging in any practical activity with others on religious grounds. Instead the issue is one of having an effective perspective at all and of having that perspective make a difference in some way in everyday practical activity. Having a religion, in the sense of assenting to traditional teachings of churches, is not difficult in the modern world, but living a religious life can be very difficult. Ambivalence over religion can disincline one from allowing a theistic perspective to permeate one's comprehension of the world or one's "take" on events; ambivalence can also keep one from taking an active part in religiously-centered or religiously-motivated activities with others.

In the contemporary world ambivalence over religion seems to arise from people developing a basic religious commitment in childhood and then becoming engrossed in non-religious endeavors during adolescence and young adulthood. The experienced world becomes divided between "macro" and "micro" institutions, with the former creating consequences for the latter but not vice-versa. Big business and big government become important and affect family, religion, and the local school. Where one lives, how well one lives, and what one does with the bulk of one's waking hours is determined by big business. Government has similar effects when it imitates big business. Family, religion, and cultural pursuits (the last of these seldom developed beyond childhood thresholds associated with local schools) become "private" matters to be left at home. People develop the habit of suppressing familial, religious, and aesthetic expressions in the course of much of their daily lives. Relationships with others are supposed to be smooth but not personal, polite but not necessarily principled, and soundtracked with piped-in mellow monotony. All this is good business. People are encouraged to "succeed" in that kind of world, exercising their talents for the benefit of business until the weekend avails them of an opportunity to restore a sense of self in "private" familial and religious activities. It should be no surprise that people feel ambivalent about taking seriously what the everyday routines of living suggest should be marginal. For such ambivalence to be overcome, people need to make an object of it, examine its origins and forms, and criticize the social structure that engenders it.

By the time people are "older" adults, they have become marginalized into retirement and become ambivalent about themselves.

In general they are also no longer involved at all in one of the "micro" institutions - local education. When children grow up and leave home, the family comes to be reduced to two people and is in danger of existing at all if one of the spouses takes seriously ill or dies. The one institution that can provide the framework for life *through* all this is religion, but to be effective it needs to be present in an effective way through all of this, not merely *after*. We need to consider the church ministries to older people in the light of this larger situation. This means that we need to consider how "micro" institutions can be effective. There seem to be several general approaches or stratagems for institutional effectiveness.

One of the stratagems that we saw churches employing in their ministries to older persons was helping people contend with the "macro" institutions. Older persons' fellowship groups organized workshops on such matters as finances, Medicare, and insurance. Sometimes ministers to older people accompanied individuals to banks or meetings with attorneys and business representatives. It should not be surprising if older persons who have developed expertise in dealing with one or more kinds of micro institution share much of that knowledge informally over coffee in a church meeting room. By helping older people deal with big business and government, the churches play an important role in practical affairs without themselves being part of the "macro" structure that is marginalizing people.

More often, the churches follow a second stratagem wherein they supplement family and friendship group activities. Setting up visitation programs, providing transportation, supplying meals, organizing entertainment events, arranging for household repairs, and other such activities amount to undertakings that normally occur in families and friendship groups for younger people. Referring people to mental health specalists is a service that is often performed by church personnel for congregation members of all ages, but it is also done by family members. When the churches organize activities for older persons as well as when it helps people avail themselves of mental health services, it is operating within the "micro" institutional context. One of the important aspects of the churches' presence in the micro or marginal settings in modern society is its availing all members, including the less educated and lower income members, the advice and perspective of the minister to older persons; this person, whether lay or clergy, is usually a relatively educated and experienced individual who can bring an informed perspective to people's problems that often cannot be found among the members of a family or friendship group.

A third stratagem entails organizing older persons into service activities. Under religious auspices the individual does not really disengage from society but instead works in a service capacity. The service may take the form of specifically worship-related activities such as conducting religious educational sessions or singing in the choir, or it may be a matter of visiting or assisting other older congregation members who are home bound or incapacitated. The service may also take the form of out-reach endeavors to help the homeless, feed the hungry, and collect clothing and furniture for the needy. Such activities are clearly work, but they are done not for pay but because they are worth doing in themselves.

We can suggest some lines of future development in ministries to and by older church members, lines that would be natural extensions of what is being done already. First, if the churches are going to involve people in addition to those who had been church activists all along, they need to address the problem of ambivalence over religion. For many people, there is a need for religion to shed the trappings of the nursery. A religion that is built on an authoritarian subculture may help keep children in line, but it can be a barrier to the more broadly experienced adults. Specifically, a morality that is based on what good things people can do rather than on what rules they should not violate is one that can actually motivate people's involvements in providing service. Moreover the various Christian traditions have rich intellectual and spiritual heritages that can appeal to adults who want to develop themselves beyond the religiosities they knew in childhood. Holding people back to a religious populism might have satisfied a market for the weekend quick fix at a point in time when few people lived beyond retirement and beyond loss of family role, when fewer yet had much energy at an advanced age, but the situation has changed and promises to change further. The ranks of the older people who are also healthy are growing; many of them have educations and experiences that have developed in non-religious endeavors; there is no reason why they shouldn't develop equally in religious endeavors. It is a bizarre anomaly for someone to have the religion of a fourteen-year-old and, for example, and at the same time have a career and a Master's-level education in business or some technical field. Education programs in the history of religions, literary approaches to the Bible, religious art, and traditions of spirituality seem to be a logical preliminary to church involvement, a preliminary that can overcome ambivalence over religion by making the religiosity of the individual as advanced as the individual's accomplishments in the world of big business or government.

Second, it would appear natural for churches to organize businesses that can be run as collectives, using the employee-owned business as a model. Part-time jobs for older people need not be fragmentary experiences that are disconnected from any social network; they can be run by such networks. From bookstores and computer software retailers to insurance and rental agencies, there are many lines of work that can be organized around the availability of older people rather than around the typical corporate structure. Just as churches first organized educational and medical institutions with the betterment of society in mind, they can organize new ways of engaging in business. Such an effort can become particularly important when it becomes necessary for both public and private pension plan to delay providing benefits to ages greater than sixty-five. Precisely because churches are not at the center, because they are not embodiments of a macro institution in the modern world, they can depart from established ways of doing things and provide new organizational models.

Notes

[1] In Christian tradition, these two dimensions of religion are expressed in the tradition of the two great commandments; see Mark 12.29-31 and its parallels, Matthew 22.36-38 and Luke 10.27.

Appendix One

Religion Moderating Depression

In Chapters 3 and 4, I present a number of tables supplied by Baqar A. Husaini that report information from an interview study conducted in 1990 among 995 elderly residents (498 whites and 497 African Americans) of Nashville, Tennessee. The data were collected under NIH (MBRS) grant S06-RR08092-16 - Baqar A. Husaini principal investigator. Because this volume is intended for the general reader rather than specialists, I limited the analysis in the two chapters to simple tables that the generally educated reader can understand. However, by using procedures that only people who have some background in statistics can interpret, it is possible to combine the information contained in the many tables into one summary table and achieve a more rigorous and refined analysis. The purpose of this appendix is to present the more advanced analysis for readers who have an understanding of multivariate statistical analysis. This is the analysis that actually guided us in our presentation in the two chapters; it will be reported in a forthcoming article by Baqar A. Husaini, Oscar Miller, and myself.

The respondents were interviewed in a follow-up study to a previous survey that had been conducted two years earlier with an original panel of 1,200 randomly selected respondents (600 whites and 600 African Americans). Both waves of data collection (1988 and 1990) focused on relevant information, but only the 1990 data are used in the present analysis. The data concern demographic characteristics, chronic medical problems, some aspects of religiosity, social networks and social support, and depression. The chronic medical problems were measured by an extensive check list. An indicator of social stressors consisted of summed scores representing questions about stressful life events and financial problems. Items concerning religion were only included in the 1990 interviews. Public religiosity was measured by combining frequencies of church attendance and involvement in other religiously-sponsored activities. Private religiosity was measured by a sum of frequency scores of a variety of other activities - Bible reading, praying only in times of crisis and need, listening to religious broadcast programs, talking about religious topics with friends and family, and trying to convert someone.[1] Depression symptoms were measured with the widely-used CES-D scale.[2]

Table A-1 reports some relevant means and percentages for the variables that proved to be important in the analysis. Because many of these measures differed significantly by racial category, separate analyses were needed for the African American and white subsamples. It is also the case that the original study was designed to enable the research team to make cross racial comparisons; that is why the two racial subsamples are equal in size rather than representative of the racial composition of the Nashville metropolitan area (which was 83.09 white and 15.47 African American in 1990).[3]

The statistical model that best explains the CES-D (depression symptom) scores has two stages. In the first stage the measures of public religiosity, private religiosity, medical problems, and social stress are regressed on the measure of perceived social support. Public religiosity was a statistically significant positive predictor and medical problems a statistically significant negative predictor of perceived social support in the white subsample while private religiosity and medical problems were both statistically significant positive predictors of perceived social support in the African American subsample (see Table A-2). It may well be that public religiosity varied more among the white subsample and private religiosity more among the African American subsample, making these relevant independent variables for predicting perceived social support; that does not mean, of course, that public religiosity did not occasion perceived social support for the African American respondents, only that it did not predict it. The fact that private religiosity predicted perceived social support in the African American subpopulation can be explained by the interview item referring to talking to friends and family about religion; the item indirectly indicated levels of contact with friends and family.

In the second stage of the analysis, measures of public religiosity, private religiosity, medical problems, social stress, and social support are regressed on the CES-D depression symptom scores. In "Model 2" (see Table A-3) public religiosity appears to buffer the effects on depression symptom scores of the two stressors (medical problems and social stress) for the white subsample (though not at a statistically significant level) while private religiosity appears to do so for the African American subsample. "Model 3" shows that perceived social support, which the first stage of analysis showed to be an effect of public religiosity for whites and private religiosity for African Americans, buffers the effects of the stressors on depression symptoms, causing all of the independent effects of public religiosity among the whites and much of the independent effects of private religiosity among the African Americans to "wash out." Some of the independent (i.e., not explained by social support) buffering effect of private religiosity among the African Americans remains.

Table A-1: Mean Scores of Principal and Demographic Variables By Race

Variable	White (N=498)	African American (N=497)
Principal Variables		
Depression (CES-D)	5.03	4.48
Public Religiosity	2.04	2.52*
Private Religiosity	5.83	6.98*
Number of Medical Problems	4.64*	3.85
Social Stressors	2.49*	2.28
Perceived Social Support	20.88	21.62*
Demographic Variables		
Age	72.79	71.87
Education (years)	10.55*	9.15
Females	82.6%	71.0%
Married	23.6%	26.6%

*Higher score significant at .05 level

Table A-2: Standardized Regression Coefficients
(Dependent Variable = Perceived Social Support)

Independent Variables	Whites	African Americans
Public Religiosity	.19*	.10
Private Religiosity	.07	.18
Medical Problems	-.10*	.18*
Social Stress	.03	.02
R2	.18	.08

*Significant at .05 level

Table A-3: Standardized Regression Coefficients
(Dependent Variable = Depression Symptoms)

Independent Variables	Model 1 Whites	Model 1 Blacks	Model 2 Whites	Model 2 Blacks	Model 3 Whites	Model 3 Blacks
Public Religiosity	-.16**	.03	-.12	.04	-.03	.06
Private Religiosity	-.10**	-.06	-.08	-.14**	-.09*	-.10*
Medical Problems			.29**	.23**	.26**	.21**
Social Stress			.18*	.34**	-.18**	.34*
Social Support					-.27**	-.17**
R2	.05	.03	.18	.20	.24	.22

*Significant at .10 level
**Significant at .05 level

Appendix Two

Sample and Method in the Study of Ministers to the Elderly

Lists of the largely African American Christian congregations and of the largely white Christian congregations of Nashville, Tennessee, and the immediately surrounding area (Davidson County and communities bordering it) and lists of their pastors were drawn up with the assistance of local informants, by consulting directories, and when necessary by means of Sunday morning observations. Census tract information for 1990 was looked up for the census tracts in which church buildings were located and the tracts in which the published home addresses of their principal clergy were located. A randomized one fourth sample was drawn from the lists and the selected pastors or other ministers to older persons contacted for interviews. Potential respondents rarely declined to be interviewed straightforwardly, but sometimes they asked repeatedly to be contacted at a later date, ostensibly because of their busy schedules. In cases where a pattern of repeatedly not being available for an interview occurred, the next church on the list was substituted, and if necessary the one after that. The churches were listed alphabetically within denominations. Because the larger more prosperous churches had full time office staff and were easier to contact, the substitution of churches was not pursued too far, lest the less prosperous churches with no one normally available to answer the church phones be under represented in the sample. When repeated efforts to contact someone at the church by phone failed, attempts were made to call pastors at their homes to set up interviews. This approach generally succeeded and thus avoided the necessity of leaving out some of the smaller churches that did not have secretaries available to answer phones.

Sixty-one pastors or other ministers to the elderly from largely African American congregations were interviewed, mostly during the winter of 1997, and 133 pastors or other ministers to the elderly from the largely white congregations were interviewed from the spring of 1997 through October of the same year; there was also a largely Latino congregation represented in the sample. We grouped the congregations statistically into three types of Christian religious tradition, based on the denominational affiliation or, if independent, their self-description - charismatic (including the Church of God, Pentecostal, Holiness, and Assembly of God denominations), conservative (including Baptists of various kinds, Seventh-day Adventist, Southern Methodist, Churches of Christ, Jehovah's Witness, the Missouri and Wisconsin Lutheran synods, and the Nazarene denominations), and an "other" grouping of liturgical and liberal churches (including Christian Science, Evangelical Lutheran Church in America, Episcopal, Catholics, Presbyterians, Unitarian, United Methodists, United Church of Christ, and Disciples of Christ). Fifteen (8.11%) of the congregations were from the charismatic denominations, 106 (57.30%) from the conservative ones, and 47 (25.41%) from the "other" category. An additional 17 (9.19%) were non-denominational or independent and unclassifiable.

We used a questionnaire schedule that elicited, among other items of information, the formal educational attainment of the respondents, estimates of the congregational attendance on a typical Sunday (or Saturday, in the case of the Seventh-day Adventists), estimates of the number of congregation members aged 65 years of age and above, how many of these elderly had come to them or spoken with them during the previous working month with mental, emotional, or nerve problems, and whose advice the respondents might seek if an elderly congregation member seemed especially tense, distressed, depressed, or even suicidal. We also asked what kinds of problem those who came or spoke with them had, what they did in response, and if they referred anyone to a specialist or other person what kind of professional (or other relevant category) the person to whom they referred the individual was. We also recorded mentions the respondents volunteered about any programs generally for or by the elderly that were maintained in their congregations.

The following tables present descriptive data by denomination on the total population of known congregations, whether or not they were included in our sample. Table A-4 lists the denominations of the largely white congregations in the order of the mean per capita income levels of the census tracts in which the church buildings are located, all as reported by the 1990 U.S. Census. Table A-5 is a similar presentation of the largely African American congregations. Table A-6 lists the denominations of the largely white congregations in the order of the mean per capita incomes of the census tracts in which their senior pastors' reside, again based on the 1990 U.S. Census. Table A-7 is a similar presentation of the largely African American congregations. The class standings of denominations sometimes vary from one urban area to another; readers should refer to these tables rather than their experiences in other locations for an overview of the denominational stratification of the Nashville metropolitan area, from which our sample was drawn.

Table A-4: 1990 Per Capita Income of Church Census Tracts
Predominantly Majority Congregations

	Mean Per Capita Income	Number of Congregation
Episcopal	23,566	
Presbyterian - Cumbrlnd	14,789	9
Churches of Christ	14,674	85
Jehovah's Witness	14,092	8
Baptist - Free Will	13,855	18
Apostalic	13,429	1
Nazarene	13,371	26
Seventh Day Adventist	13,270	2
Church of God	12,902	8
Pentecostal	12,802	21
Baptist - General	12,732	3
Catholic	12,011	13
Baptist - Independent	11,658	28
Mormon	11,315	3

Table A-5: 1990 Per Capita Income of Church Census Tracts
Predominantly African American Congregations

	Mean Per Capita Income	Number of Churches
Presbyterian - USA	11,858	2
Independent	10,711	14
Presbyterian	10,408	1
Church of God in Christ	9,112	9
Methodist - United	9,032	11
Baptist - Missionary	8,529	83
Presbyterian - Cumbrlnd	8,440	4
Church of God	8,134	7
Baptist	8,101	16
Baptist - Primitive	8,029	18
Pentecostal	7,930	9
Seventh-Day Adventist	7,857	2
Apostolic	7,777	6
Churches of Christ	7,751	7
Catholic	7,626	1
Christian Methodist Ep.	7,300	5
African Methodist Ep.	7,293	12
Disciples	6,826	2
United Church of Christ	6,595	1
Episcopal	6,178	2
Lutheran - E.L.C.A.	5,802	1

Table A-6: Mean Per Capita Income of Census Tracts
of Pastors' Residences
(Predominantly White Congregations - Total Known Population)

Denomination	Pastor's Tract Per Capita Income	N*
United Church of Christ	31,254	2
Lutheran - E.L.C.A.	27,639	3
Methodist - Southern	25,234	2
Episcopal	24,550	6
Christian	23,862	3
Presbyterian - U.S.A.	23,244	2
Independent	20,664	4
Disciples	19,755	3
Methodist - United	19,545	24
Lutheran - Mo & Wis	17,943	3
Wesleyan	17,332	2
Baptist - Southern	17,297	44
Nazarene	16,892	8
Church of Christ	16,577	31
Assemblies of God	15,476	4
Baptist - Free Will	14,158	7
Pentecostal	13,503	5
Catholic	13,178	11
Church of God	13,112	3
Interdenominational	12,903	3
Presbyterian - Cumberland	12,606	3
Baptist	12,101	10

*Cases of only one known pastor's residence in a denomination deleted.

Table A-7: Mean Per Capita Income of Census Tracts of Pastors'
Residences
(Predominantly African American Congregations - Total Known
Population)

Denomination	Pastors' Tract Per Capita Income 1990	N*
Methodist - United	14,384	8
African Methodist Episcopal	14,121	9
Apostolic	13,127	5
Baptist	12,321	13
Churches of Christ	11,775	3
Baptist - Missionary	11,047	61
Baptist - Primitive	11,003	11
Church of God in Christ	10,719	4
Independent	10,027	9
Christian Methodist Episcopal	10,019	3
Pentecostal	8,493	6
Church of God	8,482	2

*Cases for only one known pastor's residence in a denomination are deleted.

Notes

[1]We are fully aware of the limitations of both of these measures. However, they are what is available in the data set for a secondary analysis.

[2]L.S. Radloff, "The CESD Scale: A Self-Report Depression Scale for Research in the General Population," *Applied Psychological Measurement* 1:3 (1977): 385-401.

[3]Calculated from U.S. Bureau of the Census, *1990 Census of Population and Housing. Nashville, TN MSA* (Washington: U.S. Government Printing Office, 1993).

Index of Names and Sources

Adams, P.F., 13
Adkins, Sharon, vi

Beeglehole, R., 21
Berger, Peter L., 55
Blasi, Anthony J., 41, 65, 103
Bradley, Martin B., et al., 92
Brouard, N., 21

Caselli, G., 21

Diamond, Timothy, 20
Drumwright, Darnell A., v
Dykstra, P.A., 21

Emerson, Janice, v

Fanshel, D., 21
Fulton, John Peter, 12

Glenmary Research Center, vi, 92

Hardy, William, vi
Health Care Financing Administration, 20, 21
Horvath, Tibor, 54
Husaini, Baqar A., v, 21, 35, 36, 37, 38, 39, 40, 41, 49, 50, 51, 52, 103

Kahoe, Richard D., 55
Koenig, Harold G., 5
Kutner, B., 2

Landis, Benson Y., 93
Langer, T.S., 21
Lopez, A.D., 21
Luckmann, Thomas, 66

McKinlay, J.B., 21
McKinlay, S.M., 21

Malinowski, Bronislaw, 55
Marano, M.A., 13
Mathers, C., 21
Meadow, Mary Jo, 55
Miller, Oscar, 41, 103
Mills, C. Wright, 65

National Center for Health Statistics, v, 11, 21
National Health Interview Survey (1984), 11

Radloff, L., 41, 113
Robine, J.M., 21
Rubenstein, R.L., 55

Strickland, Mary, vi

Tam Lung, Joseph, v-vi
Togo, A.M., 21

U.S. Bureau of the Census, v, 2, 3, 5, 6, 7, 8, 11, 12, 19, 20, 21, 92, 113

Weaver, Andrew J., 55
Weigert, Andrew J., 65

Index of Topics

Activity, 45, 47, 48, 55, 64, 97-98

Advertising, 1

Advisor to minister to older persons, 87-88

African Americans, 50, 52, 55, 56, 104ff.

Altruism, 44

Ambivalence, 57ff., 99, 101-02

Assistance, needs for, 4

Assisted living facilities, 14

Alcohol, 3

Baby boom, 3

Barriers to religious involvement, 53-54

Bathing, 13

CES-D scale, 33, 41, 104ff.

Charismatic denominations, 71, 76, 79, 70, 87, 108

Charitable works, 44-45, 83

Church community, 46ff.

Church membership, 17, 78

Class, social, 26-29

Class culture, 88, 90

Community, 62-64
    See Network

Congregation, 46-47, 78, 79
    Size of, 84

Connectedness in church organization, 76ff.

Conservative denominations, 71, 76, 79, 87, 108

Conversion experience, 59

Denominations, 68ff.

Depression, 14-15, 18, 32-33, 35ff., 41, 49, 50, 52, 53, 56, 65, 67, 98, 104ff.

Disability, 10

Disability benefits, 8

Disengagement, 2,3

Diet, 3

Elder (church official), 93

Employment, 8, 9

Environments, 23

Exercise, 3

Faith, 21, 47

Family, 15, 48

Family problems, 80, 81

Family role, 96

Family values, 27

Fellowship groups, 83

Finances, 4-9, 32, 34, 36-37, 81

Financial management, 11, 12

Gendered roles, 26ff.

God imagery, 58

Grief, 15, 83-84

Health, 10-15, 32, 33-34, 36, 50, 80, 81

Health expectancy, 10, 95

Home health care, 14

Householders, 3

Housework, 11, 12

Housing, 3, 4

Imagination, 23-24

Income per capita, census
    tract, 70, 81
Individualism, 63
Institution, social, 59-60
    Macro, 60, 61, 63, 99, 100
    Micro, 60, 61, 99-100
Insurance, 4
Interest income, 8

Liberal denominations, 76
Life cycle, 2, 95
Life expectancy
    See Longevity
Liturgical denominations, 76
Loneliness, 15, 35, 48, 95
Longevity, 3,4,10

Magic, 46, 53, 55
Managed care, 4
Marginality, 59-62, 99
Master status, 63
Meals, 83
Medicaid, 19-20
Medical establishment, 3, 16
Medical expenses, 4, 36, 37
Medical problems
    See Health
Medicare, 5, 16, 19, 20, 95, 96
Ministers to older persons, 49,
    84ff., 100
Ministry by older persons, 64-
    65, 78, 82-83, 101

Nashville, 9, 16, 18, 33, 34,
    35, 36, 37, 38, 39, 49, 51,
    67ff., 103ff., 107ff.
Networks, 17, 26, 37, 28, 29,
    47, 48, 51, 53, 63, 80, 86,
    96, 98

New York City, 10
Nursing homes, 3, 12-14, 19-
    20

Older people
    Health of, 3
    Living alone, 6-7
    Marginalization of, 2
    Population size, 2-3
    Resources of, 16-17

Presented, 23ff.
Plausibility structure, 47, 55
Poverty level, 5-6
Prayer, 45, 47, 53
Private sphere of life, 61
Problems, 31ff., 80-81
Public health, 3

Quality of life, 3, 4, 15, 32, 33,
    35, 44, 53

Referrals to specialists, 49, 53,
    89, 90
Religion
    adult, 59
    as an activity, 44, 48
    as a resource, 43ff.
    capacity for, 24, 96
    definition of, 21, 35
    extrinsic, 55
    importance of, 16, 40
    intrinsic, 55
    private, 46, 51, 52, 53,
        55, 67, 98, 103-4
    public, 46, 49, 50, 51, 52,
        53, 55, 98,3, 104
Religious perspective, 43ff.,
    53, 67, 97

Rental income, 8
Representativeness, 70-71
Retirement, 96

Seek rate, 86-87
Self concept, 58, 61
Self-care limitations, 11, 12,
     14, 32
Shopping, 11, 12
Social integration, 17
Social Security, 5, 8, 20, 95,
     96
Social support, 17, 38-40, 45,
     50, 51, 52, 53, 56, 63, 67,
     98, 104ff.
          Perceived social
          supportscore, 35
Spirituality, 18, 21, 53, 61, 96
SSI, 8
Stress, 9, 15, 32, 58, 103, 104
Structure of society, 59

Tobacco, 3

Ultimate concern, 44, 45, 54-
     55

Veterans' benefits, 8
Visitation programs, 82

Well-being
     See Quality of life
Wisdom, 17
Work role, 26, 27, 28, 31-32,
     48, 63, 96, 102